DREAM KEYS

A Guide For First-Time Home Buyers

By

Zee Pressley

Disclaimer: All "true(ish)" stories in this book are fictional and meant to teach, not to disclose. While they're inspired by real-life situations, any names, details, or coincidences are purely for laughs and learning. These stories are here to guide, not diagnose—so always connect with a licensed Realtor*, lender, or legal pro when making your real-life moves. In short: Learn from the lessons, but live your own story.*

Table Of Contents

Dream Keys

"Your dream keys don't just open doors—they open up freedom, fun, and all the good life ahead."

Introduction

WHY IS REAL ESTATE SUCH A BIG DEAL AMONG THE WEALTHY?

Real estate has long been the top investment choice among the wealthy, offering stability, appreciation, and control. Unlike stocks, it's a tangible asset that generates passive income, provides powerful tax advantages, and acts as a hedge against inflation. With the ability to leverage other people's money, build long-term wealth, and pass down a lasting legacy, real estate stands as a proven path to financial freedom and generational success.

When weighing the pros and cons of buying a home, there's one big question to ask yourself… How long do I want to donate to someone else's wealth? Take a look at the scenario below:

Jeane signed her lease on March 1, 2022. She paid a $2200 deposit and $2200 for the first month's rent, totaling $4,4,00.

She loved her rental and remained there for two years. She not only loved her rental but was also very generous in sending her landlord, Mr. Igotmine, and his family on a beautiful vacation along the pink sand beaches of Bermuda, sponsored by the rental income they received from Jeane.

Mathing the Math: $2200 deposit + $2200/month X 2 years = $56,800 was her total contribution to the Igotmine family. Imagine if Jeane had used that $4,400 towards her own home.

Benefits of homeownership – you invest in your Stability and Security. When you own your home, you decide when you want to move on.

True(ish) Story: Learning the Hard Way

Louis was a neighbor of mine who had been a faithful lessee of Mr. Igotmine for 7 years. While sitting at the dinner table one tranquil and insouciant evening, the Igotmines were deliberating how they would fund young Steven's 4 years of college at Texas A&M. After all, young Steven had to become an Aggie too. They wanted young Steven to enjoy his college years, so they would not dare have him work; thus, he would need a hefty allowance and a car.

After a few dinner meetings between Mr. and Mrs. Igotmine, it was decided that they would sell the home Louis was so comfortably leasing. They were kind enough to give her a 60-day notice, but since Louis was not much of a saver, she didn't have enough money saved to pay the deposit and rent on her new dwelling. Fortunately, Louis's friend Lisa owned a home in a nearby community and was kind enough to allow her friend Louis to stay with her while she saved enough money to lease another home.

Bye-bye stability and security when you are the leasee. Your residence's owners can sell at their will and for any reason they please.

FINANCIAL AND PERSONAL ADVANTAGES- YOU INVEST IN YOUR WEALTH.

When you own your home, you decide when, where, and how much you want to invest.

True(ish) story: The 25-year-old with Vision

I knew this student once, Lisa, who was only 25 years old when she purchased her first home. It was a bit of a fixer-upper, but Lisa wasn't afraid of putting in a little bit of elbow work to make the home to her liking.

Lisa's home was 1200 sq ft. It had a separate living and dining space, 3 bedrooms, and 2 baths. It also had a cute little front porch, which was why Lisa fell in love with the home.

Lisa, being from New Orleans, loved to entertain, but that living room just didn't give her the airy feeling she desired. Lisa decided to invite Louis, Ronnie, and a few other friends over for a "Wall Be Gone" party. The gang had a wonderful time eating, sipping, and slamming the mallet through the wall.

The next day, Lisa's uncle Ray came by and, in just a few hours, Lisa's small living room opened grandly as part of the dining area, allowing her the open plan she couldn't afford with one of those newer homes.

You see, vision was all it took for Lisa to find a home in an area she desired, at a price she felt comfortable with. And enough space to house her friend Louis for a while.

Modifying her space also increased the desirability of her home, making it a charming fit for today's market. Lisa's home equity increased several thousand dollars over the past 10 years. She pulled a few grand from the equity of her home and paid cash for the car she'd been longing to buy.

Chapter 1:

Assessing Your Readiness

ARE YOU READY TO BUY?

Financial stability and readiness – If you are wondering whether you are financially stable and ready to buy a home, here are some steps you can take:

Frequently asked questions:

- How long do I have to be employed?
- Typically, most lenders prefer that borrowers be employed at least two years in the same job or industry; there are some allowable exceptions. These exceptions may include:
- Recent college graduates or licensed employees such as teachers, nurses, industry managers, police officers, and many others may qualify for a home upon receiving a letter of hire and/or a pay stub.
- Some certifications are also acceptable with proof of employment/income.
- Each situation is unique and should be evaluated by a loan officer.

Note: Lending regulations vary. It may be necessary to speak with different lenders concerning loan approval.

What do lenders look for?

Consistency, Reliability, and Stability: Why are these qualities important?

To explain why these are important, let me tell you a story.

True(ish) story: Lending like a Lender

I had a friend, Caden. Caden asked to borrow $1,000. Now, I knew Caden well, but even friendship makes you pause when money's on the line.

Here is how my thought process worked: I weighed her work history, and that is what lenders do when deciding on home loan approvals.

Caden's history looked like this:

- Caden was hired 2 months ago as a hotel manager with no prior experience.
- Caden has been working for two consecutive years as a manager for Gas-up Incorporated.

- Caden changes jobs, sometimes 2-3 times a year, going from retail, banking, and telemarketing, but she's never been out of work.

Based only on the information provided, which job best demonstrates Caden's Consistency, Reliability, and Stability?

This is a bird's-eye view of what lenders may consider. Of course, they would dig deeper into Caden's work history, credit, and banking resources before deciding on Caden's qualifications.

- Lifestyle considerations – We want what we want.
- We like what we like.
- With home shopping being at your fingertips, it's easy to become consumed with pre-shopping (Putting the cart before the horse). If preshopping is a means of motivating, then shop away. However, it's best to know your buying power so that you can shop within an affordable range. Here are a few reasons why knowing your buying power is crucial.
- Once you see a home you like, it will be challenging to settle for anything less.

- If you have used a home-buying calculator, taxes and insurance are specific to the area, which may skew our calculations.
- Mortgage rates vary.
- These are just a few reasons why it is in the buyer's best interest to get a loan approval before preshopping. Speak with a Realtor or Lender before pre-shopping.
- Long-term vs. short-term plans – Remember, most Real Estate is built on a concrete slab; however, your loan is drafted on paper, which means that even if your first home is not your long-term desire, you can sell (cash-in) and use the equity you have accumulated toward a future home purchase, or begin building a portfolio of rental properties.

CHAPTER 1 TAKEAWAY:

Before you start house-hunting, take a power pause—check your job history, talk to a realtor or lender, and get clear on what you can actually afford. Skip the guessing game and know your numbers! Remember, your first home doesn't have to be forever—it just needs to be a smart step. Think of it as your launchpad to build equity, grow wealth, and open even bigger doors in the future.

"Ready, set, know your power — because the smartest buyers don't just find keys, they unlock futures."

Dream Keys Notes

Chapter 2:

Financial Preparation

UNDERSTANDING YOUR FINANCES – LEAVE THE NUMBERS TO THE PROFESSIONALS

True(ish) story: Yelin, Mitch, and the Backyard Wedding Dream

Yelin and Mitch, two friends of mine, were newly engaged and dreaming big. They imagined getting married right in the backyard of their first home. Yelin had been working at Foot Locker for three years and was juggling online business classes on the side. Mitch had just finished nursing school and landed his first job as an Oncology R.N. at M.D. Anderson. Life felt like it was lining up just right.

One weekend, they took a drive through Yelin's parents' neighborhood. The neighborhood was quiet, and they both absolutely loved it. That's when they spotted a house they could make home. It was at 2100 Perfect Lane with a **for sale** sign in the yard. That's where they knew where they wanted the wedding to be.

They called their agent, who had suggested that they get approval before shopping. As a committed agent, she met them at the property and gave them a grand tour. They were in love. Their realtor asked that they contact their lender as soon as possible. They did. They learned that the homes' flood insurance, homeowners' insurance, taxes, and interest rates elevated the cost of the home out of their financial reach.

It was challenging to find a home in their price range, but fortunately, with the assistance of their Lender and Realtor, they found a home just a few miles outside of Yelin's parents' neighborhood, and they lived happily ever after.

Lesson: Speak with your Realtor or Lender before pre-shopping. They want to be a part of making your home-buying experience a pleasant one.

- Saving and budget planning are key to ensuring that you are financially fit to purchase a home.
- Understanding credit scores and how to improve them is important. Our Lender can often point you in the right direction.

- Determining how much house you can afford is the most important factor in pursuing the home search. Know what you can buy before you shop.
- They are closing cost and downpayment assistance programs that can assist in making our home dreams come true. You will learn more about First Time Home Buyer Programs in the upcoming chapters.

CHAPTER 2 TAKEAWAY:

Money talks, but your lender and Realtor translate! Don't guess—get the facts. Before you fall for the front porch of your dreams, sit down with a pro to see what's truly in your financial reach. Create a budget, learn your credit score, and ask about assistance programs. You don't have to do it alone—team up early, plan smart, and turn your dream into a doable reality.

"Don't fall in love with a home before you fall in line with your finances!"

Dream Keys Notes

Chapter 3:

Mortgage Basics

TYPES OF MORTGAGES

Fixed-rate vs. adjustable-rate mortgages: Fixed rates are a homeowner's best bet. A fixed rate is locked from the date you sign your agreement until the final payment.

This is one of the great advantages of buying a home. Where rent can fluctuate from year to year or month to month, a fixed mortgage can offer a buyer the ability to plan based on agreed mortgage terms. This may raise the question, "What is a good rate?" It depends on the market. Currently (2024), the average mortgage rate is between 6%-7%, which may seem a bit high from rates we have seen in the past, particularly those of 2020-2021, where rates plummeted to an all-time low of 1.78 – 2.78% being average, of course, based on many factors.

When it is time to buy a home, interest (mortgage) rates are often the driving factor in whether or not to purchase a home. Here's the good news. In today's market, builders, mortgage companies, and sellers are aware of this market tight-hold, which is why many of them offer assistance in buying down rates.

Waiting to purchase a home when the rates go down can potentially cost you more, because as rates go down, home prices may go up.

Here's a story.

True(ish) Story: The Waiting Game

Back in 2021, I came across a couple, Mr. and Mrs. Savvy, who were interested in buying a home. Like a lot of buyers at the time, they were shocked by how quickly prices had climbed. Even though they were preapproved at an interest rate of 2.98%, they hesitated.

Their thinking was understandable: "If we wait a bit, prices will come down. We don't want to buy at the top."

So they waited.

Fast forward, a year later (2022), and both home prices and interest rates rose. They were so distraught that they lost the zeal to purchase.

Many factors drive interest rates. A common misconception is that if a friend of a friend was offered a 5.99% interest rate, that would be the rate for all. Credit and other factors determine the rate; thus, rates are based on an individual's profile.

Note: There is an option to lower rates by buying down rates, if feasible.

EXAMPLE:

Scenario: FHA 30-Year Fixed Mortgage:

Home Price: $350,000

Down Payment (3.5%): $12,250

Base Loan Amount: $337,750

Upfront MIP (1.75%): $5,911.13 (rolled into loan)

Total Loan Amount: $343,661.13

OPTION A: NO BUYDOWN

Interest Rate: 7.0%

Monthly Principal & Interest: $2,287

Monthly MIP (0.55% annually): ~$157

Total Monthly Payment: $2,444

OPTION B: BUY DOWN THE RATE

Buy 1 Discount Point (1%): $3,377.50

New Interest Rate: 6.5%

Monthly Principal & Interest: $2,171

Monthly MIP (same): ~$157

Total Monthly Payment: $2,328 **Considerations:**

- Improve Credit and Reduce Debt

  Better credit = better rates. Pay down debt and avoid new credit before applying for a mortgage.

- Set a Realistic Budget and Down Payment

  Know what you can afford beyond the purchase price—include closing costs, reserves, and monthly expenses.

- Get Pre-Approved and Compare Loan Options

  Pre-approval gives buying power. Explore FHA, VA, or Conventional loans to find the best fit for your goals.

DECISION

When considering how much to put down on your above the standard 3.5% FHA and 3% Conventional:

What to consider when putting more than the minimum down on a home:

- Lower Monthly Payments

  A bigger down payment reduces your loan and monthly costs.

- Mortgage Insurance Savings

  Put 20% down on a conventional loan to avoid PMI and save money monthly.

- Keep Cash Reserves

  Don't drain your savings—budget for emergencies, repairs, and moving costs.

- Think Long-Term

  More down makes sense if you plan to stay long-term. Less may be smarter if you'll sell or refinance soon.

- Consider Opportunity Cost

  Extra cash could be invested elsewhere— don't overlook growth potential.

What are Adjustable Mortgage Rates (ARM)? When might they be beneficial? Short-term homeownership or plan to refinance.

Plan to Move Soon: If you plan to sell the home or refinance before the adjustable period starts (typically 5, 7, or 10 years), you can benefit from the lower initial interest rate without facing the risk of rate adjustments.

Lower Initial Payments

Lower Initial Rates: ARMs usually offer lower initial interest rates compared to fixed-rate mortgages. This can result in lower initial monthly payments, freeing up cash for other expenses or investments.

True(ish) Story: The Savers' Smart Bet on an ARM

I knew a couple once, Mr. and Mrs. Saver, who had their eyes on a new construction home. It was the kind of home they once thought was out of reach. But in 2023, mortgage rates were hovering close to 7%, and that dream looked like it might slip away.

Then their lender presented an option: a 3.75% adjustable-rate mortgage (ARM). That rate, nearly three points lower than the 30-year fixed, significantly reduced their monthly payment.

After reviewing the risks and the timeline, the Savers went for it.

Mr. and Mrs. Saver agreed to refinance and obtain a fixed-rate mortgage as they study market trends and seize the opportunity to secure a 5% refinance option within the first 3-4 years. This option to accept the 3.99% ARM saved them money for the first few years of homeownership; however, no crystal ball determines the direction rates will go.

An ARM may appear to be a good idea; however, consider budgeting for an increased rate of 2 percent or more in the event the market does not go down.

GOVERNMENT-BACKED LOANS (FHA, VA, USDA)

FHA loans are mortgages insured by the Federal Housing Administration, designed to help people buy homes with lower down payments and easier qualification requirements. Here's a simplified overview:

They are good for those who need lower down payments and have less-than-perfect credit, but consider the extra cost of mortgage insurance and property standards.

EXAMPLE

For a $200,000 home with a 3.5% down payment:

- Down Payment: $7,000

- Loan Amount: $193,000
- Upfront MIP: $3,377.50 (can be added to the loan)
- Annual MIP: Approximately 0.85% of the loan amount, divided into monthly payments.

KEY FEATURES

- Low Down Payments:

  Minimum down payment is 3.5% of the purchase price.

- Lower Credit Score Requirements:

  Minimum credit score of 580 for the 3.5% down payment option.

  Scores between 500 and 579 may qualify with a 10% down payment.

- Easier Qualification:

  Higher debt-to-income ratios allowed.

  More lenient on employment history and income.

- Mortgage Insurance:

  Upfront Mortgage Insurance Premium (UFMIP): 1.75% of the loan amount.

Annual Mortgage Insurance Premium (MIP): Paid monthly, varies based on loan amount and term.

- 5. Loan Limits:

  Varies by area based on local housing costs.

Benefits

- Easier to qualify with lower credit scores and higher debt.
- Low down payment of 3.5%.
- Assumable loans make it potentially easier to sell your home.

Drawbacks

- Requires both upfront and annual mortgage insurance.
- Homes must meet certain property standards.
- Loan limits may not cover higher-priced homes.

Who Should Consider an FHA Loan?

- First-time homebuyers.
- People with lower savings for down payments.
- Those with lower credit scores.

- Buyers with a higher debt-to-income ratio

VA loans are mortgages backed by the U.S. Department of Veterans Affairs, designed to help veterans, active-duty service members, and eligible surviving spouses buy homes. Here's a simplified overview:

VA loans are great for eligible veterans, active-duty service members, and surviving spouses due to no down payment, no PMI, lower interest rates, and flexible credit requirements. Be aware of the funding fee and property standards

KEY FEATURES

- No Down Payment:

  You can buy a home with no down payment.

- No Private Mortgage Insurance (PMI):

  No PMI is required, even with no down payment.

- Lower Interest Rates:

  VA loans often have lower interest rates.

- Flexible Credit Requirements:

  Easier to qualify with lower credit scores.

- Limited Closing Costs:

  The VA caps the amount you can be charged for closing costs.

- No Prepayment Penalty:

  You can pay off the loan early without penalties.

BENEFITS

- Save Money Upfront: No down payment and no PMI.
- Lower Monthly Payments: Competitive interest rates and no PMI.
- Easier to Qualify: More flexible credit requirements.
- Early Payoff: No penalty for paying off the loan early.

DRAWBACKS

- Funding Fee: A one-time fee that can be added to the loan.
- Primary Residence Only: Must be your primary home, not an investment property.
- Property Standards: The home must meet VA standards.

Eligibility

- Who Qualifies: Veterans, active-duty service members, and eligible surviving spouses.
- Proof of Eligibility: A Certificate of Eligibility (COE) is required.

Example

For a $250,000 home with no down payment:

- Loan Amount: $250,000
- Funding Fee: 2.3% for first-time use ($5,750), can be added to the loan.
- Monthly Payment: Lower because there's no PMI and often lower interest rates.

Who Should Consider a VA Loan?

- Veterans and Active-Duty Service Members: Those eligible based on military service.
- First-Time Homebuyers: Veterans with limited savings.
- Those with Lower Credit Scores: Easier qualification.

- Refinancing: Good options for refinancing existing loans.

USDA loans: USDA loans are mortgages backed by the United States Department of Agriculture.

(USDA) aimed at helping low- to moderate-income borrowers in rural and some suburban areas buy homes.

USDA loans are a good choice for buyers in eligible rural and suburban areas with moderate incomes. They offer benefits like no down payment, lower costs, and easier qualifications. Make sure you meet the location and income requirements before applying.

Key Features

- No Down Payment:

  You can buy a home with no down payment.

- Low Mortgage Insurance:

  USDA loans have lower mortgage insurance premiums compared to FHA loans.

- Competitive Interest Rates:

  Often lower than conventional loans due to government backing.

- Flexible Credit Requirements:
  Easier to qualify with lower credit scores.

Benefits

- Save Money Upfront: No down payment required.
- Lower Monthly Payments: Competitive interest rates and lower mortgage insurance premiums.
- Easier to Qualify: More flexible credit requirements.
- No Prepayment Penalty: You can pay off the loan early without penalties.

Drawbacks

- Geographic Restrictions: Must be in eligible rural or suburban areas.
- Income Limits: Borrowers must meet income eligibility guidelines, usually 115% of the median income for the area.
- Mortgage Insurance: Requires an upfront guarantee fee and an annual fee (paid monthly).

Eligibility

- Location: The property must be in a USDA-eligible rural or suburban area.
- Income: Household income must not exceed the limits set for the area.
- Credit: Generally, a minimum credit score of 640 is required, but this can vary.

EXAMPLE

For a $200,000 home:

- Loan Amount: $200,000
- Upfront Guarantee Fee: 1% of the loan amount ($2,000), which can be added to the loan.
- Annual Fee: 0.35% of the loan amount, paid monthly ($200,000 x 0.35% = $700 annually, about $58.33 per month).

WHO SHOULD CONSIDER A USDA LOAN?

- Rural and Suburban Homebuyers: Those looking to buy in eligible areas.
- Low- to Moderate-Income Borrowers: Those who meet the income requirements.

- First-Time Homebuyers: Ideal for those with limited savings for a down payment.
- Lower Credit Scores: More flexible qualification criteria.

USDA loans are great for eligible rural and suburban homebuyers with low to moderate income, offering no down payment, competitive interest rates, and lower mortgage insurance costs. Ensure you meet the geographic and income eligibility requirements before applying.

USDA loans are mortgages backed by the U.S. Department of Agriculture, aimed at helping low- to moderate-income buyers in rural and some suburban areas purchase homes. Here's a straightforward overview:

Key Features

- No Down Payment:

  Buy a home without needing a down payment.

- Lower Mortgage Insurance:

  USDA loans have cheaper mortgage insurance compared to other loans.

- Competitive Interest Rates:

  Often lower than conventional loans due to government support.

- Flexible Credit Requirements:

  Easier to qualify with lower credit scores.

Benefits

- Save Money Upfront: No down payment required.
- Lower Monthly Costs: Competitive rates and cheaper mortgage insurance.
- Easier Qualification: More flexible credit rules.
- No Penalty for Early Payment: Pay off the loan early without extra fees.

Drawbacks

- Geographic Limits: Only available in eligible rural or suburban areas.
- Income Limits: Must meet income guidelines, usually up to 115% of the area's median income.
- Mortgage Insurance Fees: Includes an upfront guarantee fee and an annual fee.

Eligibility

- Location: Property must be in a USDA-approved rural or suburban area.
- Income: Household earnings must fit within set limits.
- Credit: Typically requires a minimum credit score, usually around 640.

Example

For a $200,000 home:

- Loan Amount: $200,000
- Upfront Guarantee Fee: 1% of the loan amount ($2,000) can be added to the loan.
- Annual Fee: 0.35% of the loan amount ($700 annually, about $58.33 per month).

Who Should Consider a USDA Loan?

- Rural and Suburban Buyers: Anyone looking in eligible areas.
- Lower to Moderate Incomes: Those who fit income limits.
- First-time buyers: Especially with little saved for a down payment.

- Lower Credit Scores: More forgiving requirements.
- Getting Pre-Approved

The pre-approval process: The pre-approval process is the first step toward homeownership. This step separates the dreamers from the conquerors. Dreamers wish, hope, and imagine themselves in a home. Conquerors take action steps toward making their dream a reality.

In my 18+ years of experience, I have not met anyone who doesn't desire to own a home. My experience has been that they either don't believe they can or have not been educated on where to begin the process and what's required to earn our keys.

Note: There are no magic tricks or shortcuts. It takes dedication and commitment. Remember, someone who has never met you wants to risk loaning hundreds of thousands of dollars to you. Certainly, your professional and financial profile must be worth the risk.

The reality of homeownership is possible for ANYONE who dares to take the necessary steps to conquer their dream. On average, a plan takes from 1 to 12 months.

True(ish) story: First class to First Closing

I joined a Real Estate company within 48 hours of passing my Real Estate Exam. The company I joined enrolled me in a 30-day training program. On the 30th day, I gave my first Home Buyers class. That class led to my first client closing on a home in 30 days. Facilitating my first Home Buyer's Class sparked a journey of educating the public on the home-buying process, resulting in homeownership for many generational renters.

I had discovered my niche. Within 3 years, I placed 90 families in homes. My clients are from a pool of fast-food workers, department stores, clerical, management, military, and independent contractors. Some had credit issues, and some lacked closing funds, but together we conquered obstacles and made their home dreams a reality. Today, I continue to offer home-buying classes empowering people to invest in themselves.

Getting Pre-approved: Start by understanding your credit score and finances. There are many options to obtain a free report. Evaluate your finances. Then gather documents, choose a lender, complete the application, and submit your documents for review.

If you run into a credit roadblock, a good lender or realtor can refer you to help.

Once you have reviewed your credit score and secured at least one to two years of employment within the same industry, you are well on your way.

Chapter 3 Quiz: Test Your Mortgage Knowledge

- What is the main advantage of a fixed-rate mortgage?

  It usually has lower initial payments.

  The interest rate stays the same throughout the loan.

  It allows you to refinance anytime without penalty.

- When might an adjustable-rate mortgage (ARM) be a smart choice?

  If you plan to sell or refinance before the adjustable period starts.

  If you want to lock in a rate for 30 years.

If you don't care about budgeting for payment changes.

- Why is it important to improve your credit before applying for a mortgage?

  Better credit means you qualify for higher loan amounts.

  Better credit usually leads to lower interest rates and monthly payments.

  It has no impact on mortgage rates.

- What is one benefit of putting at least 20% down on a conventional loan?

  You get a longer loan term.

  You can avoid paying private mortgage insurance (PMI).

  You don't need to get pre-approved.

- Why should you get pre-approved before house hunting?

  It tells you exactly how much home you can afford.

  It guarantees you'll get the lowest interest rate.

  It's not necessary; you can just shop around first.

Answer Key

1-b, 2-a, 3-b, 4-b, 5-a

"Know your mortgage mojo—because guessing costs more than just money."

Dream Keys Notes

Chapter 4:

The Home Buying Process

STEP-BY-STEP GUIDE

Building Your Home Buying Team:

Who are the players on your team?

REALTOR (BUYER'S AGENT)

Your trusted guide throughout the home-buying journey.

- Helps you find the right home
- Writes and negotiates offers
- Coordinates inspections, appraisals, and closing
- Advocates for your best interest every step of the way

LENDER (LOAN OFFICER)

Your financing expert.

- Reviews your credit, income, and savings
- Provides loan pre-approval

- Explains loan types and monthly payments
- Starts the loan process and submits your file for processing

PROCESSOR

Your paperwork coordinator.

- Gathers and organizes documents (pay stubs, W-2s, tax returns, bank statements)
- Orders title, appraisal, and homeowners' insurance
- Coordinates verifications (employment, assets) and third-party items
- Prepares your file for underwriting and helps clear document requests

THE LOAN DECISION-MAKER.

- Verifies all financial documents
- Ensures loan guidelines are met
- Approves the loan or requests additional documentation
- Gives the final go-ahead for funding

HOME INSPECTOR

Your eyes on the home's condition.

- Examines the structure, roof, plumbing, electrical, HVAC
- Identifies needed repairs or safety concerns
- Provides a detailed inspection report
- Helps you decide whether to move forward or negotiate repairs

APPRAISER

The home's value expert.

- Determines the fair market value of the home
- Compares the property to similar recent sales
- Ensures the price matches the home's true worth
- Helps the lender avoid over-financing

Finding a real estate agent: Today, it's as simple as a click of a button or a ride down a street to find a home; however, it is essential to remember that this is likely the most significant investment you will make in years to come. Seeking professional help can ensure that you are making a safe and wise investment.

The role of a Real Estate Agent is not to just find you a home. Today, with the ease of technology, you can likely and will likely guide them to the house of choice. Real Estate Agents often have connections with lenders who may have resources that can save you thousands of dollars, as well as home inspectors, market relationships with builders, roofers, electricians, and other professionals required to ensure the health of your home.

True(ish) Story: Credit race between Brothers

I met a guy who was an independent contractor. He had a small concrete company and earned a comfortable living. However, due to limited knowledge of how credit works, his score was in the low 500s. His brother, who owned a similar service, had a similar financial profile, nice income/poor credit. Within 3 months, they raced to reset their credit profiles, and both purchased homes within 3-4 months of our goal. Knowing is half the battle.

Searching for homes: Searching for a home is the easy part. You and your agent can plan tours, attend open houses, or view available homes online. Don't be alarmed if your agent isn't as excited as you are about the aesthetics of the home. As you admire the cabinets, flooring, and other amenities, her/his focus is likely on home value and protecting your investment. Agents focus on the current and potential value of the home, negotiating the cost, and work closely with home inspectors to ensure that your home investment is worth the cost.

Attending open houses and private showings; It's a good idea to attend open houses and private showings; however, when touring, be sure to inform the seller/builder that you are working with an agent. This protects the agents from possible assumption of client representation.

Myth: If you don't use an agent, you can save money or get a better discount. Nothing could be further from the truth. Both private sellers and builders generally prefer working with agents. Agents are skilled in negotiating and have been trained in understanding the process. Think of it as having a professional advocating on your behalf. Your agent works for you. Your interest is at the forefront of the plan.

CHAPTER 4 TAKEAWAY: BUILD YOUR DREAM TEAM AND OWN YOUR JOURNEY

Buying a home isn't a solo game — it's a team sport! Get to know your Realtor, lender, processor, underwriter, inspector, and appraiser. Ask questions, stay involved, and keep communication open. When you understand each role, you take control, avoid surprises, and make your home-buying journey smoother and smarter. Remember: your dream home depends on a strong team—and you're the captain.

🗨 "Your home-buying squad is only as strong as the captain steering the ship—so suit up and lead like a boss!"

Dream Keys Notes

Chapter 5:

Making an Offer

CRAFTING THE OFFER – UNDERSTANDING YOUR BUYING POWER

- Understanding market value

  Market Value is the estimated amount for which a property should be exchanged between a willing buyer and a willing seller.

- Factors Influencing Market Value

  Location: Properties in prime locations typically have higher values.

  Condition: Well-maintained properties tend to have higher market values.

  Size and Layout: Larger properties or properties with better layouts often command higher prices.

  Amenities: Proximity to amenities such as schools, parks, shopping centers, and public transportation can increase value.

Market Conditions: Supply and demand dynamics, interest rates, and economic conditions affect market values.

- Comparable Sales

  Comparative Market Analysis (CMA): Reviewing recent sales of similar properties in the area helps establish a realistic market value. CMAs are often available through your Realtor.

  Adjustments: Differences in property features, condition, and location need to be adjusted to make accurate comparisons.

- Appraisals

  Professional Appraisal: An independent appraisal provides an unbiased estimate of a property's market value.

  Bank Appraisals: Lenders often require appraisals to ensure the property's value supports the loan amount.

- Market Trends

Price Trends: Understanding whether prices are rising, falling, or stable can guide timing and strategy.

Inventory Levels: The number of available properties can indicate whether it's a buyer's or seller's market.

Days on Market (DOM): Properties that stay on the market longer may be overpriced, while those selling quickly may indicate strong demand.

- Negotiation Leverage

Knowledge of Value: Knowing the market value helps buyers negotiate better deals and avoid overpaying.

Offer Strategy: Making offers based on thorough market analysis can lead to more favorable terms.

Time on the market: A negotiating tool often used by realtors. When a home has been on the market for more than 60 days, sellers are more likely to be open to adjusting their price or adding additional amenities.

Personal Properties such as appliances, drapes, or furniture may also be negotiated to make a deal more attractive to the buyer.

- Market Indicators

  Interest Rates: Lower interest rates often increase buyer affordability and demand, driving up prices.

  Economic Factors: Employment rates, consumer confidence, and economic growth can impact real estate markets.

  Scarcity of homes in a particular area: When available homes are limited in a certain area, prices may increase due to supply and demand.

  Note: Homes near major cities, offering walking distance to restaurants, shopping, medical facilities, or major tourist attractions, are often more expensive due to demand. As a rule, the further away the home is from the inner city, the lower the home price. However, new developments, resulting in the installation of utilities such as gas and electricity, generally have higher tax rates.

- Local Expertise

  Real Estate Agents: Working with experienced local agents can guide you to insights into market values and development trends specific to the area.

Community Insights: Understanding the local community's dynamics, planned developments, and zoning changes can affect future values.

- Regulatory

  Zoning Laws: Regulating property use and development can influence market values.

  Taxes and Fees: Property taxes, maintenance fees, and other costs can impact the total cost of ownership.

  MUD: Municipal Utility District provides essential services like water, sewage, and drainage to specific areas, especially in growing suburbs. A MUD, or Municipal Utility District, is a special district that provides essential services like water, sewage, and drainage to specific areas, especially in growing suburbs. Residents usually pay extra property taxes for these services, which support infrastructure funding and manage parks and streets.

  Easements are legal rights allowing someone to use a part of another person's land for specific purposes, such as power lines, cables, and the like.

> Encroachment: An encroachment is when a structure or object intrudes onto someone else's property without permission. This can include fences, buildings, or trees that extend over property lines. Encroachment is the unauthorized use of someone else's property.

True(ish) Story: The Fence, the Friendship, and the Gazebo

My neighbor and I were close, so close that we decided it would be a good idea to place an entryway in the fence that divided our backyards. This made it easy for each of us to join in backyard fun at either residence. We put a gazebo between the two homes. Then she moved. The new neighbor didn't like the idea and tore down half of the gazebo, causing the gazebo to become useless.

This story is stretched. However, we did consider it but realized what might happen if one of us moved. About a year later, she was offered a job in Dubi and moved.

In the event of encroachment, here are some possible resolutions:

Mediation can place a plan in writing that meets the needs of both parties.

- Negotiate and win-win

  Resolutions are best resolved when considering how each party is affected by the encroachment. Be fair, flexible, and firm.

- Future Projections

  Economic Forecasts: Economic trends and projections can help predict future market movements.

  Development Plans: Planned infrastructure projects, commercial developments, and other investments can enhance property values.

By understanding these aspects of market values, buyers can make more informed and strategic decisions when purchasing property.

Contingencies and clauses: Contingencies and clauses are essential components of real estate contracts that protect the interests of buyers and sellers. Here's a breakdown of each:

CONTINGENCIES

Contingencies are conditions that must be met for a real estate contract to be legally binding. If these conditions are not satisfied, the contract can be voided without penalty.

- Common Types of Contingencies:

  Financing Contingency: The sale depends on the buyer obtaining financing or a mortgage. If the buyer cannot secure a loan, they can back out of the deal without losing their earnest money.

  Inspection Contingency: The sale is contingent upon the property passing a home inspection. If significant issues are found, the buyer can negotiate repairs, request a price reduction, or cancel the contract.

  Appraisal Contingency: The property must appraise at or above the purchase price for the sale to proceed. If the appraisal is lower, the buyer can renegotiate the price or terminate the contract.

  Sale of Existing Home Contingency: The buyer's obligation to purchase is contingent on the sale of their current home. This protects the buyer from owning two homes simultaneously.

Title Contingency: The sale depends on a clear title search. Any issues with the title, such as liens or ownership disputes, must be resolved before closing.

- How Contingencies Work:

  Time Frames: Contingencies typically have specific time frames within which they must be satisfied. Failure to meet these deadlines can result in the contract becoming void or the contingency being waived.

  Negotiation: If an issue arises from a contingency, buyers and sellers can negotiate solutions, such as repairs, price adjustments, or extensions.

CLAUSES

Clauses are specific provisions included in a real estate contract to outline particular conditions or terms of the agreement.

- Common Types of Clauses:

Escalation Clause: This clause allows the buyer to increase their offer if there are competing bids by up to a specified maximum amount. It's often used in competitive markets.

Kick-Out Clause: Protects the seller when the buyer has a contingency for the sale of an existing home. It allows the seller to continue marketing the property and accept other offers. If a better offer is received, the original buyer has a certain period to remove their contingency, or the contract is terminated.

As-Is Clause: States that the property is being sold in its current condition, and the seller is not responsible for making any repairs. Buyers must accept the property without expecting improvements.

Rent-Back Agreement: Allows the seller to stay in the home for a specified period after closing, typically paying rent to the buyer. This is useful when the seller needs extra time to move.

Repair Clause: Details the specific repairs the seller agrees to make before closing. This ensures both parties are clear on what work will be completed.

- How Clauses Work:

  Customizable: Clauses can be tailored to address specific concerns or circumstances unique to the transaction.

  Legal Implications: Clauses must be carefully worded to ensure they are enforceable and clearly understood by both parties. Legal advice may be necessary to draft complex clauses.

Importance of Contingencies and Clauses

Risk Management: Contingencies protect buyers and sellers from unforeseen issues and ensure that all necessary conditions are met before finalizing the sale.

Clarity and Transparency: Clauses provide clear instructions and expectations, reducing the potential for misunderstandings or disputes.

Negotiation Tools: Both contingencies and clauses can be used as negotiation tools to address concerns and reach mutually agreeable terms.

Understanding and effectively utilizing contingencies and clauses in real estate contracts is vital for safeguarding the interests of both buyers and sellers throughout the transaction process.

Chapter 5 Takeaway: Craft Your Offer Like a Pro

Don't just throw out numbers—make your offer count! Study the market like a detective: know current trends, comparable sales (CMAs), and what's really driving prices. Use this intel to craft an offer that's competitive, smart, and tailored to your goals. Remember, the best offers aren't always the highest—they're the ones backed by strategy and confidence. Own the process and get ready to win your dream home!

"In the game of home offers, it's not just about throwing chips down—it's about playing your hand with style and smarts."

Dream Keys Notes

Chapter 6:

Inspections and Appraisals

HOME INSPECTIONS

Importance of a home inspection:

POP QUIZ: WHICH HOME DOES NOT REQUIRE A HOME INSPECTION?

- New Construction
- A friend of the family who's giving you a good deal
- A newly renovated home
- A home you purchase with cash

The correct answer is "ALL HOMES" should be inspected.

Lenders generally require a home inspection before approving a mortgage. A licensed inspection report may be necessary to ensure the property is in good condition and worth the investment. Purchasing a healthy home is key. Here are a few points that mortgage companies consider before closing a mortgage.

- Standard Practice: Lenders commonly require a home inspection to check for major issues.
- Appraisal: Lenders also require an appraisal to determine the property's market value.
- Protecting Investment: Inspections help protect the lender's investment by confirming the property is in good condition.
- Borrower Protection: Inspections help buyers by revealing potential problems and allowing for informed decisions or negotiations.

True(ish): Mr. and Mrs. Flippers purchased their first investment property. They weren't very concerned about the condition, because they expected to do some repairs. Mr. Flipper and his uncle, Toolman, decided to do the renovations themselves. Once the utilities were turned on, they realized what they thought was dirt inside the a/c vents was mold. Mold remediation was not a planned expense. They also discovered improper wiring in the primary bedroom, causing the blowout through the right side of the home. The election was another unplanned expense.

Because of the possibility of hidden defects, home purchases must be inspected by a licensed professional. The cost of professional inspection can far outweigh the cost of unplanned expenses.

Common issues and how to address them: When evaluating home concerns as a Realtor, I begin with the 5-Finger Rule.

FOUNDATION 2. ELECTRICAL 3. PLUMBING 4. HVAC 5. ROOF

Most homes, even newly developed ones, may have some concerns; however, not all concerns are deal breakers. Some problems may work to your advantage by requesting repair, replacement, or a concession.

CAUTION: Do not request a concession if you have not first estimated the repair cost and do not have a professional who can do the repair.

As some may say, "all money ain't good money." If the repair costs you more than you were awarded in the concession, you'll still have a problem.

Note: Pre-owned homes and new-construction homes generally have some form of defect. After all, they are constructed by humans, which means mistakes and oversights are possible. As such, once the home inspector has provided you with a report of suggested repairs, and the repairs have been reported as completed, it is a good idea to have your inspector reinspect to make sure that the suggested repairs have been completed to your standards. Most inspectors may charge a reduced rate to respect specific areas.

Proof of repairs: Pre-Owned homes. You may request receipts, contact information, and any warranties from the seller for home repairs that are a part of the negotiation.

New Construction Homes are often inspected by the city. In most cities/parishes, a builder must meet city compliance and pass a city inspection on the following:

Here are the most common inspections required for new construction homes:

- Foundation/Footing Inspection

  When: Before pouring concrete into the foundation,

  Purpose: To ensure that the footings and foundation are properly sized, located, and reinforced. This may also involve checking soil conditions and any grading.

- Rough Plumbing Inspection

  When: After the rough plumbing (drainage, venting, and water supply) is installed, but before walls are closed up.

  Purpose: To ensure that plumbing lines are installed correctly, without leaks, and comply with code.

- Rough Electrical Inspection

  When: After all electrical wiring, boxes, outlets, and panels are installed, but before drywall is put in place.

  Purpose: To ensure that the electrical system is properly installed and meets safety and building codes.

- Rough Framing Inspection

  When: After framing is completed and before the insulation and drywall are installed.

  Purpose: To ensure that the structure (walls, roof, floors) is properly framed, meets load-bearing requirements, and complies with building codes.

- HVAC Rough-In Inspection

When: After ductwork and HVAC systems are installed but before drywall or insulation.

Purpose: To ensure proper installation of heating, ventilation, and air conditioning systems and verify compliance with mechanical codes.

- Insulation Inspection

  When: After insulation is installed and before drywall is applied.

  Purpose: To ensure that insulation is properly installed and meets energy efficiency requirements.

- Drywall/Sheetrock Inspection

  When: After the drywall is hung but before it is taped and finished.

  Purpose: To ensure proper installation of drywall for fire safety, sound insulation, and moisture resistance.

- Final Plumbing Inspection

  When: Once all plumbing fixtures (sinks, faucets, toilets, etc.) are installed and functional.

  Purpose: To ensure that all plumbing is working correctly and complies with the final code requirements.

- Final Electrical Inspection

  When: After all outlets, lights, and electrical fixtures are installed and operational.

  Purpose: To verify the safe operation of the entire electrical system, including outlets, switches, and circuits.

- Final Building Inspection

  When: Once the construction is complete.

  Purpose: This is a comprehensive inspection of the entire structure, including windows, doors, roofing, stairs, and overall safety measures.

- Final HVAC Inspection

  When: Once the HVAC system is fully installed and operational.

  Purpose: To ensure the system works efficiently and meets code.

- Energy Efficiency Inspection

  When: Near the end of construction.

  Purpose: To ensure that the home meets energy efficiency standards, such as insulation levels, window installation, and sealing of penetrations.

- Certificate of Occupancy (CO) Inspection

  When: After all other inspections are completed and passed.

  Purpose: The city or county will issue a Certificate of Occupancy, which allows the homeowners to move in. It verifies that the house is safe, complete, and meets all building codes.

  Note: Once your home has been inspected, a copy of the inspection report and a list of requested repairs should be shared with the listing agent. The potential homeowner can discuss with the agent the mandatory repairs and negotiations that he/she require to move forward with the home sale.

  During this stage of contract negotiations, either party can agree or not agree to move forward.

  Example: If the client is requesting that all carpets throughout the home be replaced with wood flooring, the owner can honor the request or reject the option. Typically, Real Estate Agents may assist you in laying out your options, but they will not make any mandates. The decisions

APPRAISALS

Understanding the appraisal process – Prior to awarding a client a home loan, the loan officer will schedule an appraisal. The purpose of the appraisal is to determine the home's value compared to other homes in the market area. The appraisal cost is often a buyer's expense paid in advance of the appraiser appraising the home.

A home appraisal provides an unbiased, professional estimate of a property's market value. This valuation is crucial for various stakeholders and serves several important functions:

Dealing with appraisal gaps – Appraisal gaps can happen for several reasons. The more common reasons are:

- Hot Markets: Buyers offer more than the suggested sales price.
- Unique Features: Specialty property features such as an in-ground swimming pool, home theater, solar panels, and the like.

- Different Appraisals: Appraisers might value properties differently

So what happens when there is an appraisal gap? In my experience, most sellers are willing to renegotiate the price. When price negotiation isn't an option, the deal can fall through, as loan financing is based on the appraised value, not the asking price.

Covering the gap: Here are some options to cover the gap:

- Buyers can agree to pay the difference
- Have the home re-appraised

Chapter 6 Takeaway: Inspect What You Expect

Your inspector and appraiser are your home's truthtellers. Pay attention to their reports—they're not just paperwork, they're your protection plan. Use the 5 Finger Rule (Roof, Foundation, A/C, Electrical, Plumbing) to spot red flags before they become money pits. If any of those fingers point to trouble, pause and reassess. Big repairs = big costs. This is your investment—so protect it like a pro.

"If it touches the roof, runs through the pipes, cools the house, powers the lights, or holds it up—check it twice and price it right."

Dream Keys Notes

Chapter 7:

Closing the Deal

CLOSING PROCESS:

This is where your team comes together, transitioning you from dreamer to homeowner.

By this point, you have:

- Chosen a home that's right for you.
- Selected a homeowners' insurance company.
- Agreed to loan terms that fit your budget.
- Completed a home inspection and negotiated any repairs.
- Received an appraisal that meets or exceeds the purchase price.
- Completed a final walkthrough with your agent to confirm the home's agreed-upon condition.
- Received a settlement statement (Closing Disclosure) itemizing all costs and fees, including your total **cash to close** (down payment plus closing costs).

I know, I know, once you got your settlement statement, you thought it was over. Not, the underwriter may request information until you are clear about closing. This is called meeting conditions.

After conditions (any final or repeated documents, proof of funds, or any information required by the underwriter) are met, your file will be clear to close. This means:

🔍 **BEHIND THE SCENES, YOUR TEAM IS WORKING AND ENSURING THAT**

- All conditions from underwriting have been met
- Credit, income, and asset documents are verified
- The title work is clean, and the title company has reached out to you to schedule the closing
- Homeowners' insurance is in place
- Appraisal is complete and approved
- You and your Realtor have done a final walkthrough of the home

Once you are Clear To Close:

The Title Company will contact you to verify that you are aware of the amount of funds you need to close.

In most instances, cash above $1000 is not accepted. You will likely be required to provide certified funds or a wire transfer.

Chapter 7 Takeaway: Close With Confidence

You've done the work—now it's time to finish strong. Double-check your documents, stay in close contact with your lender and agent, and don't panic if the underwriter asks for one last thing (they always do!). Review your settlement statement carefully, be prepared with your certified check or wire, and celebrate your walkthrough—it's the last stop before getting your keys. The finish line is here. Show up prepared and close like a champ!

"They don't hand out keys for good intentions—you've got to show up, sign bold, and slay closing day like it's your name on the deed. Because it is."

Dream Keys Notes

Chapter 8:

Moving In

PREPARING FOR THE MOVE

As we discussed in Chapter 7, the final walk-through is a crucial step in the home-buying process. Don't skip this step. There are no takebacks after closing. The primary purpose of the walk-through is to ensure that the property is in the expected condition and that all agreed-upon repairs and contractual obligations have been fulfilled. It is typically the last opportunity for buyers to inspect the property before they finalize the transaction.

What are you looking for during your walk-through?

- Verify the Condition of the Property

  The walk-through allows buyers or renters to confirm that the property is in the same or better condition as when they last saw it, typically during the inspection or previous viewing.

It ensures that no new damage has occurred, such as leaks, broken appliances, or structural issues.

- Ensure Agreed-Upon Repairs Have Been Made

If the seller or landlord agreed to make repairs or address issues following a home inspection or rental agreement, the final walk-through confirms that those repairs have been completed as specified.

Buyers or renters should check that the repairs were done to their satisfaction and in accordance with any agreements made.

- Check that Fixtures and Appliances are Working

Order

During the walk-through, all major systems and appliances, such as heating, air conditioning, plumbing, and electrical, should be tested to ensure they are functioning properly.

Any appliances, lighting fixtures, or systems that were included in the sale or rental agreement should also be in place and working as expected.

- Confirm Removal of Personal Property

In the case of a home purchase, the walkthrough ensures that the seller has removed all personal belongings, unless otherwise agreed upon in the contract.

The property should be empty and clean, except for any items that were specifically included in the sale (e.g., furniture, appliances, or fixtures).

- Ensure Cleanliness

The property should be in "broom-clean" condition or better, meaning that it is reasonably clean, with no significant debris or clutter left behind. This is particularly important in rental situations or if it was a contractual obligation.

Buyers or renters will want to ensure that the home is ready for immediate occupancy.

- Confirm that Agreed-Upon Items are Left Behind

If certain fixtures, appliances, or personal property items were part of the purchase or lease agreement, the final walk-through ensures that these items are still in the home.

This could include things like kitchen appliances, window treatments, or built-in shelves that were agreed upon.

- Avoid Closing Surprises

For homebuyers, the final walk-through is the last chance to verify that there are no major issues before closing the deal. If there are any problems, buyers can request that they be addressed before closing or negotiate for a credit.

It provides an opportunity to avoid unpleasant surprises after the sale, as resolving problems is much harder after ownership transfers.

- Verify Utilities are Working

Utilities such as water, gas, and electricity should be turned on and functioning properly during the final walk-through. Buyers or renters should check that faucets, light switches, and heating/cooling systems are operational.

- Ensure No Unauthorized Changes

The final walk-through helps confirm that the seller or landlord hasn't made any unauthorized changes to the property, such as removing fixtures or making alterations that were not agreed upon.

- Last-Minute Negotiations

If issues are discovered during the final walk-through, it gives the buyer or renter leverage to negotiate solutions, such as repairs, compensation, or a delay in closing, before signing the final paperwork.

- Peace of Mind

Ultimately, the final walk-through provides peace of mind to buyers or renters, knowing that the property is in the condition they expect and ready for occupancy.

- Timing of the Final Walk-Through

Typically, the final walk-through occurs within 5 days before closing. This ensures there is enough time to address any requests.

The final walk-through helps ensure that all contractual obligations are met and the property is in satisfactory condition, with no unexpected issues, thereby giving buyers confidence as they finalize the transaction.

Setting up services:

Be sure to have your realtor request the names and contact information of current utility companies and other services and warranties that may be required to ensure that your home has the services it needs to function comfortably.

Setting up utilities and services – pre-owned homes generally stop services before the day of closing. Confirm when services will be disconnected and plan accordingly. New Construction often allows a three-day window for the new owner to transfer utilities. Service disconnections must be provided before closing.

Chapter 8 Takeaway: Check It Before You Close It

Before you pop the bubbly, do that final walkthrough like a boss. Check the roof to the outlets, the fridge to the faucets—because once you close, it's all yours. Use this moment to confirm repairs, test appliances, verify what stays, and ensure the home is ready for living, not fixing. Then get those utilities lined up, grab your keys, and start making that house your home.

"Do your final walk-through like a detective with a magnifying glass—because once you close, every clue you missed becomes your case to solve."

Dream Keys Notes

Chapter 9:

Homeownership Tips

MANAGING YOUR HOME INTERNAL CARE:

- First order of business is to change the locks and any security codes
- Install a security system. A door camera is inexpensive and can be installed by following a few simple directions. This will help when packages are left at your door and help identify any unsolicited visitors.
- HVAC systems must be monitored frequently for proper functioning. Check/replace air condition filters regularly. Review the recommendation, as each type may require a different service.
- Inspect Plumbing, particularly during the winter months. Be sure to wrap pipes to prevent freezing.
- Check smoke detectors. Install/replace batteries when necessary

- Place a fire extinguisher where it can be easily accessed.
- Identify where the main water value and circuits are located.
- Create a manual or electronic file and store appliance/home warranties for easy access.
- Inspect the kitchen sink disposal. To ensure freshness, a cap of bleach and or baking soda, followed by warm running water, can prevent odor.
- Do not leave food or soiled pans out overnight. If you are tired, store the soiled c/overed soiled pan/pot in the refrigerator to minimize kitchen/food orders traveling through your home.
- Periodically, use the swifter to clean and freshen walls and floors.

EXTERNAL CARE:

- Trim trees and shrubs that are too close to the home
- Water the lawn frequently to protect the shrubs and the foundation of the home

- Check windows/doors for proper sealing
- Inspect the chimney before use
- Power wash decks, patios, and outdoor furniture
- During expected bad weather, cover patio furniture or store it if expected high winds are possible
- Monitor areas that may create standing water. Standing water can be harmful if ingested by children or pets.
- Touch up paint as needed

Rodent/Insect Prevention:

Seal Entry Points:

- Use caulk and steel wool for large holes
- Trim trees to prevent squirrels from leaping onto the roof
- Monitor the home closely for possible pest entries
- Place traps near home entries
- Ultrasonic repellent devices emit high-frequency sounds that are unpleasant to rodents and may help keep them away.

- Guard your home from termites. Termites can cause extensive damage to your home.
- Inspect wooden structures regularly for signs of damage
- Check for mud tubes: termites often build mud tubes about the size of a pencil tunnel. These are often the first visible signs of termite activity
- Watch for swarmer. Liquid termiticides, professional grade, can be applied around your home; however, it is best to have your home professionally inspected if you suspect termites are present.

HOME IMPROVEMENT PROJECTS:

Plan, Save, Execute, Repeat: Home projects are never-ending. Try not to stretch your budget on a cosmetic project. Instead, plan, save, execute. Create an emergency expense account for unplanned repairs.

When in doubt, wait it out. Unless you have saved for a project, wait it out until you have put aside the resources. Owning a home can be costly; thus, planning for a rainy day is essential.

CHAPTER 9 TAKEAWAY: CARE FOR IT LIKE YOU EARNED IT (BECAUSE YOU DID!)

Homeownership isn't just a title—it's a responsibility. Protect your investment by keeping up with regular maintenance, inside and out. Change the locks, inspect your systems, stay ahead of pests, and plan for repairs before they surprise you. Create a home care routine, not a repair emergency. With a little planning, a lot of pride, and the right mindset, your home will thank you for years to come.

"You don't just live in your home—you lead it. Protect it, plan for it, and keep it shining like the dream you worked for."

Dream Keys Notes

Chapter 10:

Where's The Money $$$

Now that you understand the process, you're probably asking where the money comes from and how much you'll actually need. Good question. Many programs are available to first-time homebuyers to help with down payments and closing costs, so your out-of-pocket amount may be lower than you think.

True(ish) Story: My First Client Walked Away From Closing With Cash in Hand

My very first client was only required to bring $2200 to the closing table. Her earnest money was $2000. The Title company credited her back $200. So, yes, she walked away from closing with cash in hand.

This isn't a unique story. Using available programs, some buyers are only required to pay their down payment, and the program or seller covers the closing costs.

Of course, the price of homes has increased today since the 2006 story told above. Here's what a scenario may look like in 2025.

Home price $250K

Earnest Money = $2,500

FHA 3.5% down payment = 8,750

Earnest Money credited at closing = $2,500

Amount paid at closing, including credit = $6,250

Then, there are closing costs:

Typically, they range from 2% to 6% of the home's purchase price. Here's a breakdown of what's usually included:

TYPICAL FEES & EXPENSES INCLUDED IN CLOSING COSTS: LOAN-RELATED FEES

- Loan Origination Fee – Charged by your lender to process your mortgage (usually 0.5–1% of the loan).
- Credit Report Fee – Covers the cost of pulling your credit report.
- Underwriting Fee – Charged by the lender to assess risk and approve the loan.

Property-Related Fees

- Appraisal Fee – Required by the lender to determine the home's value.
- Home Inspection (optional but recommended) – Paid out-of-pocket before closing, not always included, but often discussed alongside.
- Survey Fee – May be required to confirm property lines (especially in rural or custom-built homes).
- Pest Inspection Fee – May be required, especially for VA loans.

Title & Legal Fees

- Title Search & Title Insurance – Ensures there are no ownership disputes or unpaid liens.
- Attorney Fees – Required in some states to review contracts and handle the closing (not required everywhere).
- Recording Fees – Charged by the county to record your deed and other legal documents.

Prepaid Costs (Escrow/Reserves)

- Prepaid Property Taxes – Your lender may require a few months of property taxes upfront.

- Homeowners Insurance Premium – You typically pay the first year at closing.
- Mortgage Insurance (if applicable) – Upfront premium for FHA loans or private mortgage insurance (PMI) on conventional loans.
- Prepaid Interest – Covers the interest between your closing date and the start of your first mortgage payment.

Additional Costs

- Real Estate Agent Commission – Usually paid by the seller, but still part of the overall transaction.
- HOA Transfer Fees or Dues – If the home is in a homeowners' association, fees may apply.

Calculating closing cost at 5% of a $250K loan, a buyer would need an additional $12,500, a grand total of $21,250

However, with the available programs, a first-time home buyer can reduce their cost by as much as 2-5% by using one of the many programs available. Here are just a few:

First-Time Homebuyer Programs:

Closing Cost & Down Payment Assistance Comparison Chart

- FHA Loan:

Down payment required: 3.5%. Closing cost help: Yes, via grants or seller credits. Who qualifies: buyers with a 580+ credit score. Key features/benefits: low credit score friendly; allows gifts and assistance programs.

- VA Loan:

Down payment required: $0. Closing cost help: Yes, via seller or lender. Who qualifies: veterans, active-duty service members, and eligible spouses. Key features/benefits: no down payment or PMI; capped closing costs.

- USDA Loan:

Down payment required: $0. Closing cost help: Yes, via seller or grants. Who qualifies: low to moderate income buyers in eligible rural areas. Key features/benefits: no down payment; low MI; property location matters.

- HomeReady (Fannie Mae):

Down payment required: 3%. Closing cost help: Yes, via grants or employer programs. Who qualifies: low to moderate income buyers with good credit. Key features/benefits: reduced MI, flexible income; allows gifts and down payment grants.

- Home Possible (Freddie Mac):

Down payment required: 3%. Closing cost help: Yes. Who qualifies: first-time and low-income buyers. Key features/benefits: low down payment; reduced MI; flexible income sourcing.

- Local/State DPA Programs:

Down payment required: varies. Closing cost help: Yes (often up to $15K+). Who qualifies: first-time buyers, income-based. Key features/benefits: may offer grants or forgivable loans for closing costs and down payment.

- Employer Assistance:

Down payment required: varies. Closing cost help: Yes. Who qualifies: employees of partner employers. Key features/benefits: may offer matched funds, forgivable loans, or closing cost support.

More About Money:

First Time Home Buyer Assistance Programs:

In Texas, various home-buying programs are available to assist first-time homebuyers, veterans, and low- to moderate-income individuals and families. Here are some key types of home-buying programs in Texas: Check your Region for Programs available to assist you.

- Texas State Affordable Housing Corporation (TSAHC) Programs:

    Homes for Texas Heroes Program: Offers down payment assistance and low-interest mortgage loans to teachers, police officers, firefighters, EMS personnel, corrections officers, and veterans.

    Home Sweet Texas Home Loan Program: Provides down payment assistance and low-interest mortgage loans for low- to moderate-income homebuyers.

- Texas Department of Housing and Community Affairs (TDHCA) Programs:

    My First Texas Home: Offers mortgage loans and down payment assistance to eligible first-time homebuyers and veterans.

Texas Mortgage Credit Certificate Program (MCC): Allows first-time homebuyers to claim a tax credit for a portion of their mortgage interest, reducing their federal tax liability.

- Local and Regional Programs:

  Many cities and counties in Texas offer homebuyer assistance programs tailored to their residents. Examples include:

  Dallas Homebuyer Assistance Program: Provides down payment and closing cost assistance to low- and moderate-income homebuyers.

  Houston Homebuyer Assistance Program: Offers financial assistance for down payments, closing costs, and prepaid expenses.

  San Antonio Homeownership Incentive Program (HIP): Provides down payment and closing cost assistance to eligible homebuyers in San Antonio.

- Federal Programs:

  Federal Housing Administration (FHA) Loans: Insured by the FHA, these loans require a lower down payment and are more lenient on credit scores.

U.S. Department of Veterans Affairs (VA) Loans: Provide veterans, active-duty service members, and their families with competitive interest rates and no down payment.

U.S. Department of Agriculture (USDA) Loans: These loans are available for rural homebuyers with low to moderate incomes, offering low interest rates and no down payment requirement.

- Non-Profit and Community-Based Programs:

  Organizations like Habitat for Humanity provide affordable homeownership opportunities through non-profit loans and sweat equity programs.

  Neighborhood Assistance Corporation of America (NACA): Offers mortgage loans with no down payment, no closing costs, no fees, and below-market interest rates.

- Employer-Assisted Housing Programs:

  Some employers offer housing assistance as a benefit to their employees. This can include down payment assistance, low-interest loans, or housing counseling services.

Each program has its own eligibility requirements, benefits, and application processes, so it's important for potential homebuyers to research and understand the specifics of each program to determine which ones they qualify for and which best meet their needs.

Quick Notes:

- Closing Cost Help: Often comes from a combination of grants, lender credits, or seller contributions.
- "First-Time Buyer" typically means no home ownership in the past 3 years.
- DPA = Down Payment Assistance
- Many programs can be layered (e.g., FHA loan + local DPA grant).

Chapter 10 Takeaway: Know the Money, Then Move with Power

You don't have to be rich to buy a home—you just have to be resourceful. Start by knowing your numbers: your down payment, your estimated closing costs, and what support is available. From federal programs to local grants, you have options. Connect with a lender who knows how to stack programs and stretch your dollars. With the right tools and a plan, you can buy with less— and sometimes even walk away from the closing table with cash in hand.

"The money is out there—you just need the right keys to unlock it. Don't let the price tag scare you; let the plan prepare you."

Dream Keys Notes

Chapter 11:

Summing Things Up

Dream Keys: Key Points Overview

Know Your Why

Homeownership starts with a vision. Define your purpose and set your intention—it's your motivation and your compass.

"When your why is clear, your path gets fearless."

Check Your Readiness

Evaluate your financial stability, employment, lifestyle, and long-term goals before jumping in.

"You don't have to be perfect to start—you just have to be prepared to move."

Understand Your Finances

Know your credit score, budget, and buying power. Speak with a lender early to build a clear, confident plan. *"Money speaks, but knowledge shouts. Own your numbers, and the keys will follow."*

Learn the Mortgage Basics

Explore loan types, interest rates, and what works best for your situation. Don't just look at the rate—look at the big picture.

"The rate matters, but the right loan unlocks your real future."

Build a Winning Team

Surround yourself with professionals—Realtor, lender, inspector, appraiser—who are committed to your success.

"You don't need to know everything—you just need the right people in your corner."

Craft Smart Offers

Study the market, lean on your Realtor's guidance, and make informed offers that reflect value, not just emotion.

"A smart offer isn't just emotional—it's strategic. Know your worth and the market."

Protect Your Investment

Inspections, appraisals, and the final walk-through aren't extras—they're essential. Know what to check and why.

"Inspections are your insurance. Protect your peace before you sign the line."

Plan Your Move with Purpose

Prep your move-in, utilities, and final walk-through like a pro. Small details = big peace of mind.

"A powerful move-in starts with preparation, not panic."

Maintain Like a Boss

Use the 5-Finger Rule (Roof, Foundation, A/C, Electrical, Plumbing), seasonal maintenance tips, and pest prevention to keep your home strong.

"You earned this home—now treat it like the investment it is."

Use the Action Plan

Chapter 12 is your personalized roadmap. Fill it in, follow it, and revise it as you go. You've got this!

"Dreams need direction. A plan turns intention into results."

Chapter 11 Takeaway: You've Got the Keys—Now Do the Work

This is where dreaming turns into doing. Everything you've learned has led to this moment. Now it's time to apply the knowledge, ask the right questions, and take ownership—literally and mentally. You're no longer guessing, you're moving with intention. The process won't always be perfect, but you are prepared. Walk it out with confidence. You've earned the keys—now own the journey.

"The dream was cute, but now it's time to handle business. You've got the keys—so turn the lock and run the block."

Dream Keys Notes

Chapter 12:

Plan Your Home Dream And Get Your Keys

CHAPTER 12: MY DREAM KEYS HOMEBUYING ACTION PLAN

Congratulations! You've made it this far—and now it's time to turn your knowledge into action. Use this worksheet to create a clear, personalized roadmap to homeownership. Dream bold, write it down, and get moving toward the keys!

STEP 1: DEFINE YOUR WHY

Why do you want to become a homeowner?

What will homeownership mean for you and your family?

____

____

2: Know Where You Stand Financially

My Current Credit Score (Estimate):

Debts I Need to Pay Down:

Savings Goal for Down Payment/Closing Costs ($):

Step 3: Set Your Budget

Target Monthly Mortgage Payment ($):

Estimated Total Price Range ($):

Step 4: Build Your Dream Team

Lender/Bank Contact:

____

Realtor/Agent Contact:

____

Inspector/Appraiser/Other Pros:

____

____

Step 5: Visualize Your Dream Home

Target Area/City/Zip Codes:

____

____

Must-Haves (Top 3):

____

____

Nice-to-Haves (Bonus Features):

____

____

____

STEP 6: TIMELINE TO BUY

Ideal Move-In Date: ___________________________

Steps I Will Take This Month:

____

____

Support I Need:

____

____

Dream Keys Notes

Glossary of Terms

1. Appraisal – A professional estimate of a property's market value, often required by lenders.
2. Closing Costs – Fees paid at the end of a real estate transaction, including lender fees, title insurance, and taxes.
3. Contingency – A condition in a purchase contract that must be met before the deal can close (e.g., inspection, financing).
4. Down Payment – The amount of money a buyer pays upfront, typically 3%–20% of the home price.
5. Earnest Money – A deposit made to show a buyer's serious intent to purchase; applied toward closing costs.
6. Equity – The difference between what your home is worth and what you owe on it.
7. Escrow – A third party that holds funds or documents until the transaction is complete.
8. FHA Loan – A government-backed mortgage requires as little as 3.5% down, which is ideal for first-time buyers.

9. Fixed-Rate Mortgage – A loan with an interest rate that stays the same over the life of the loan.
10. Home Inspection – A professional evaluation of the home's condition before purchase.
11. Listing Agent – The real estate agent who represents the seller.
12. Loan Estimate (LE) – A breakdown of the estimated costs and terms of a mortgage loan.
13. PMI (Private Mortgage Insurance) – Insurance required for conventional loans with less than 20% down.
14. Pre-Approval – A lender's written commitment showing how much a buyer is qualified to borrow.
15. Principal – The amount borrowed on a mortgage, not including interest.
16. Property Taxes – Annual taxes paid to the local government based on property value.
17. Title – Legal ownership of a property.
18. Underwriting – The lender's process of reviewing financial information to approve a loan.
19. VA Loan – A zero-down loan option for eligible veterans and military service members.

20. Walkthrough (Final) – A last look at the home before closing to ensure it's in the agreed-upon condition.

POWER WORDS:

Settlement Statement: - Describes who pays what, and what is due or given at closing.

Clear-To-Close: You've completed the underwriting process, and your file is ready for funding.

Congratulations, future homeowner! Buying your first home can feel overwhelming at times, but remember: you don't have to be perfect, just prepared to take action. You've got the tools, the mindset, and the motivation to take that next bold step toward owning your future.

If you're ready to turn all this knowledge into keys in your hand, connect with a trusted Realtor who can guide you through the process, answer your questions, and help you buy with power and confidence. You don't have to do this alone—reach out today and make homeownership happen!

Welcome to Your Dream Keys Toolkit

Congratulations! You've taken in the knowledge, boosted your mindset, and now it's time to take powerful, informed action. This section is where dreams meet paper.

Inside this appendix, you'll find sample forms, checklists, and tools designed to help you navigate each step of the homebuying journey. From budgeting and loan comparisons to mortgage readiness and closing documents, these pages are here to guide and support you like your favorite real estate coach (that's me!).

Pro Tip: Feel free to copy, print, highlight, and revisit these tools often. They're meant to move with you—not just sit pretty at the back of a book.

You've got the keys. Now, go unlock that door.

Zee

Appendix Table of Contents

Sample Closing Disclosure Page 1 Summary

For Educational Purposes Only

Property: 456 Home Sweet Ln, Hometown, ST 12345

Buyer: Jane Doe

Loan Type: FHA 30-Year Fixed

Closing Date: August 15, 2025

Loan Amount: $245,000

Loan & Transaction Details

Sales Price $250,000

Down Payment $5,000

Earnest Money Deposit $1,500

Seller Credit $2,000

Cash to Close (Final) $11,995

Buyer's Closing Costs

Loan Origination Fee $1,000

Appraisal Fee $550

Credit Report Fee $45

Flood Certification $20

Title Insurance $850

Settlement Agent Fee $500

Recording Fees $200

Prepaid Property Taxes $900

Homeowners Insurance $1,200

Daily Interest (13 days) $375

Escrow Reserves $1,500 Total

Buyer Closing Costs $7,140

SUMMARY – BUYER'S SIDE

Total Due from Buyer at Closing $257,140

Less Loan Amount $245,000

Less Earnest Money $1,500

Less Seller Credit $2,000

Final Cash to Close $11,995

Pro Tip: Your Closing Disclosure must be given to you at least 3 business days before closing.

Review it line by line with your lender or agent. Don't hesitate to ask questions!

First-Time Home Buyer Budget Worksheet

MONTHLY INCOME

Source	Amount
Primary Job	$_____
Side Hustle Part-Time	$_____
Child Support/Alimony	$_____
Other Income	$_____
	$_____

TOTAL MONTHLY INCOME

MONTHLY EXPENSES

Category	**Estimated Amount**
Rent Mortgage (Current)	$_____
Utilities (electric, gas, water) 3	$_____
Internet Phone	$_____
Groceries Food	$_____
Transportation (gar, car note)	$_____
Car Insurance	$_____

Health Insurance $_____

Subscriptions Streaming $_____

Credit Card Payments $_____

Student Loans $_____

Childcare School Expenses $_____

Other $_____

Total Monthly Expenses $_____

HOME BUYING SAVINGS GOALS

Goal Target Amount Saved So Far Monthly Contribution

Down Payment $_____

Closing Costs $_____

Emergency Fund (1-6 months) $_____

Moving Costs $_____

Furniture Appliances $_____

Total Home Buying Goal $_____

MONTHLY BUDGET SUMMARY

Summary Category	**Amount**
Total Income	$_____
Total Expenses	$_____

Summary Category	**Amount**
Total Saved Toward Home	$_____

Remaining Balance $_____

NOTES & ADJUSTMENTS

Use this space to reflect on ways to cut back or increase savings

markdam

Coppadit

____

____

____

____

____

Mortgage Readiness Checklist

Use this checklist to prepare for the mortgage preapproval and application process. Check off each item as you complete it.

1. Credit Score Review

- I have reviewed my credit report from all three bureaus (Experian, TransUnion, Equifax)
- I know my current credit scores are:
  Experian: ________ **TransUnion:** ________
  Equifax: ________
- I have disputed any errors on my credit report.
  Comments: ___________________________
- I have paid down or paid off high-interest debt
  Notes: _________________________________
- I understand how my credit score affects loan approval and interest rates

Notes:

____

2. Pre-Approval Documentation

Gather the documents most lenders will ask for:

Document Type	**Ready?**	**Notes**
Government-issued ID (Driver's License, Passport)	[ ]	
Social Security Number/ITIN	[ ]	
Last 2 Years of Tax Returns	[ ]	
Last 2 Years of W-2s or 1099s	[ ]	
Last 2–3 Months of Pay Stubs	[ ]	
Bank Statements (Checking/Savings)	[ ]	
Proof of Any Additional Income	[ ]	
Gift Letter (if receiving funds from family)	[ ]	

3. Employment Verification

- I have been employed for at least 2 years in the same field
- My income is steady or increasing

- I can provide employer contact information for verification
- I have documents for recent job changes (offer letters, contracts, etc.)

4. Bank Statements & Assets

- I have saved for a down payment: **$**__________
- I have an emergency fund (3–6 months of expenses)
- I have documentation of all large deposits
- I understand the difference between liquid funds and retirement accounts

Notes & Next Steps

Use this space to jot down questions, action steps, or deadlines:

Markdown

CopyEdit

____

____

____

____

PROMULGATED BY THE TEXAS REAL ESTATE COMMISSION (TREC)

EQUAL HOUSING OPPORTUNITY

THIRD PARTY FINANCING ADDENDUM

TO CONTRACT CONCERNING THE PROPERTY AT

1. TYPE OF FINANCING AND DUTY TO APPLY AND OBTAIN APPROVAL: Buyer shall apply promptly for all financing described below and make every reasonable effort to obtain approval for the financing, including but not limited to furnishing all information and documents required by Buyer's lender. (Check applicable boxes):

A. CONVENTIONAL FINANCING:

(1) A first mortgage loan in the principal amount of $____________ (excluding any financed PMI premium), due in full in ________ year(s), with interest not to exceed % per annum for the first ________ year(s) of the loan with Origination Charges as shown on Buyer's Loan Estimate for the loan not to exceed % of the loan.

(2) A second mortgage loan in the principal amount of $ (excluding any financed PMI premium), due in full in ________ year(s), with interest not to exceed % per annum for the first ________ year(s) of the loan with Origination Charges as shown on Buyer's Loan Estimate for the loan not to exceed % of the loan.

B. TEXAS VETERANS LOAN: A loan(s) from the Texas Veterans Land Board of $ for a period in the total amount of _______ years at the interest rate established by the Texas Veterans Land Board.

C. FHA INSURED FINANCING: A Section _______ FHA insured loan of not less than $_____ (excluding any financed MIP), amortizable monthly for not less than _______ years, with interest not to exceed ___% per annum for the first _______ year(s) of the loan with Origination Charges as shown on Buyer's Loan Estimate for the loan not to exceed % of the loan.

D. VA GUARANTEED FINANCING: A VA guaranteed loan of not less than $ (excluding any financed Funding Fee), amortizable monthly for not less than _______ years, with interest not to exceed ___% per annum for the first _______ year(s) of the loan with Origination Charges as shown on Buyer's Loan Estimate for the loan not to exceed % of the loan.

E. USDA GUARANTEED FINANCING: A USDA-guaranteed loan of not less than $ (excluding any financed Funding Fee), amortizable monthly for not less than _______ years, with interest not to exceed ___% per annum for the first _______ year(s) of the loan with Origination

Charges as shown on Buyer's Loan Estimate for the loan not to exceed % of the loan.

F. REVERSE MORTGAGE FINANCING: A reverse mortgage loan (also known as a Home Equity Conversion Mortgage loan) in the original principal amount of $ (excluding any financed PMI premium or other costs), with interest not to exceed ___% per annum for the first _______ year(s) of the loan with Origination Charges as shown on Buyer's Loan Estimate for the loan not to exceed % of the loan. The reverse mortgage loan will will not be an FHA insured loan.

G. OTHER FINANCING: A loan not of a type described above from (name of lender) in the principal amount of $ due in _______ year(s), with interest not to exceed _______% per annum for the first _______ year(s) of the loan with Origination Charges not to exceed _______% of the loan. Buyer does does not waive all rights to terminate the contract under Paragraph 2B of this addendum for the loan described in this paragraph.

APPROVAL OF FINANCING: Approval for the financing described above will be deemed to have been obtained when Buyer Approval and Property Approval are obtained. **Time is of the essence for this paragraph and**

strict compliance with the time for performance is required.

Initialed for identification by Buyer ________ ________ and Seller ________ ________

A. BUYER APPROVAL (Check one box only):

[X] This contract is subject to Buyer obtaining Buyer Approval. If Buyer cannot obtain Buyer Approval, Buyer may terminate this contract within 21 days after the Effective Date of the contract by giving Seller: (i) notice of termination; and (ii) a copy of a written statement from the lender setting forth the reason(s) for lender's determination. If Buyer terminates the contract under this provision, this contract will terminate and the earnest money will be refunded to Buyer. If Buyer does not terminate the contract under this paragraph, Buyer Approval will be deemed to have been obtained when (i) the terms of the loan(s) described above are available and (ii) lender determines that Buyer has satisfied all of lender's requirements related to Buyer's assets, income and credit history.

[ ] This contract is not subject to Buyer obtaining Buyer Approval.

B. PROPERTY APPROVAL: If Buyer's lender determines that the Property does not satisfy lender's underwriting requirements for the loan (including but not limited to appraisal, insurability, and lender required repairs), Buyer may terminate this contract on or before the 3rd day before the Closing Date by giving Seller: (i) notice of termination; and (ii) a copy of a written statement from the lender setting forth the reason(s) for lender's determination. If Buyer terminates under this paragraph, the earnest money will be refunded to Buyer. If Buyer does not terminate under this p.aragraph, Property Approval is deemed to have been obtained.

3. SECURITY: If required by Buyer's lender, each note for the financing described above must be secured by vendor's and deed of trust liens.

4. FHA/VA REQUIRED PROVISION: If the financing described above involves FHA insured or

VA financing, it is expressly agreed that, notwithstanding any other provision of this contract, the purchaser (Buyer) shall not be obligated to complete the purchase of the Property described herein or to incur any penalty by forfeiture of earnest money deposits or otherwise: (i) unless the Buyer has been given in accordance with HUD/FHA or VA requirements a written statement issued by the Federal Housing Commissioner, Department of Veterans Affairs, or a Direct Endorsement Lender setting forth the appraised value of the Property of not less than or (ii) if the contract purchase price or cost exceeds the reasonable value of the Property established by the Department of Veterans Affairs. The 3-day notice of termination requirement in Paragraph 2B does not apply to this Paragraph 4. $

A. The Buyer shall have the privilege and option of proceeding with consummation of the contract without regard to the amount of the appraised valuation or the reasonable value established by the Department of Veterans Affairs.

B. If FHA financing is involved, the appraised valuation is arrived at to determine the maximum mortgage the Department of Housing and Urban Development will insure. HUD does not warrant the value or the condition of the Property. The Buyer should satisfy himself/herself that the price and the condition of the Property are acceptable.

C. If VA financing is involved and if Buyer elects to complete the purchase at an amount in excess of the reasonable value established by the VA, Buyer shall pay such excess amount in cash from a source which Buyer agrees to disclose to the VA and which Buyer represents will not be from borrowed funds except as approved by

VA. If VA reasonable value of the Property is less than the Sales Prices, Seller may reduce the Sales Price to an amount equal to the VA reasonable value and the sale will be closed at the lower Sales Price with proportionate adjustments to the down payment and the loan amount.

Buyer For Educational Pruposes ONLY: ___________

Seller For Educational Purposes ONLY: ___________

Buyer: ___________

Seller: ___________

TREC

This form has been approved by the Texas Real Estate Commission for use with similarly approved or promulgated contract forms. Such approval relates to this form only. TREC forms are intended for use only by trained real estate license holders. No representation is made as to the legal validity or adequacy of any provision in any specific transactions. It is not intended for complex transactions. Texas Real Estate Commission, P.O. Box 12188, Austin, TX 78711-2188, (512) 936-3000 (http://www.trec.texas.gov) TREC No. 40-11. This form replaces TREC No. 40-10.

TEXAS REAL ESTATE COMMISSION

Produced with Lone Wolf Transactions (zip Form Edition) 717 N Harwood St, Suite 2200, Dallas, TX 75201

www.lwolf.com

Kayla Carter

TREC
TEXAS REAL ESTATE COMMISSION

The form of this contract has been approved by the Texas Real Estate Commission. TREC forms are intended for use only by trained real estate license holders. No representation is made as to the legal validity or adequacy of any provision in any specific transactions. It is not intended for complex transactions. Texas Real Estate Commission, P.O. Box 12188, Austin, TX 78711-2188, (512) 936-3000 (http://www.trec.texas.gov) TREC NO .20-18.This form replaces TREC NO.20-17.

Loan Program Comparison Chart

Feature / Loan Type	**FHA**	**Conventional**	**USDA**	**VA**
Minimum Down Payment	3.5%	3% (first-time buyers)	0%	0%
Credit Score Requirement nt	580+ (500 w/ 10% down)	620+	640+	No official minimum (usually 620+)
Mortgage Insurance	Required (Upfront + Monthly MIP)	Required if <20% down (PMI)	Required (annual fee)	None
Income Limits	None	None	Yes – income limits apply	No income limit
Location Restrictions	No	No	Yes – must be in an eligible rural area	No

Feature / Loan Type	FHA	Conventional	USDA	VA
Eligible Property Types	Primary residence only	Primary, secondary, investment	Primary residence only	Primary residence only
Best For	Low credit scores, small down payments	Good credit, flexible terms	Rural buyers with low to moderate income	Veterans, active duty, and eligible spouses
Closing Costs Assistance	Allowed via seller/assistance programs	Allowed	Allowed	Allowed

Notes:

___

___

___

___

Quick Guide: Understanding Home Types & Builder Incentives

When buying a home, it's helpful to understand the three most common categories: resale homes, newly built homes, and new construction inventory homes. Each one comes with different expectations, timelines, and potential perks.

PRE-OWNED / RESALE HOMES

- **Definition**: Previously lived-in homes sold by private sellers.
- **Expectations**:

  More flexible negotiation on price and repairs

  May need updates or inspections

  Seller contributions to closing costs vary

  Often ready to move in right away

New Construction (Build from the Ground Up)

- **Definition**: Buyer selects lot, layout, and finishes; builder constructs the home.

- **Expectations**:

  Longer build timeline (4–12 months)

  Modern design and energy efficiency

  Builder incentives may include design upgrades or closing costs

  Usually, you must use the builder's preferred lender to receive incentives

Inventory / Spec Homes

- **Definition**: A new home already built or nearly finished, offered by a builder.

- **Expectations**:

  Quick move-in (typically 30–60 days)

  Often includes builder incentives like:

  Closing cost assistance

  Appliance packages

  Interest rate buy-downs

  Less customization, but everything is new

BUYER TIPS:

- Always **ask about builder incentives**—they change monthly or by promotion.
- Using the **builder's preferred lender** may unlock major savings, but always compare loan offers.
- Bring your **own buyer's agent** to advocate for you (builder reps work for the builder).

PROMULGATED BY THE TEXAS REAL ESTATE COMMISSION (TREC)

ONE TO FOUR FAMILY RESIDENTIAL CONTRACT (RESALE)

NOTICE: Not For Use For Condominium Transactions

1. **PARTIES**: The parties to this contract For Educational Purposes ONLY (Seller) and For Educational Pruposes ONLY (Buyer). Seller agrees to sell and convey to Buyer and Buyer agrees to buy from Seller the Property defined below.

2. **PROPERTY**: The land, improvements and accessories are collectively referred to as the Property (Property).

A. LAND: Lot 26 Block 5, Sample Street Addition, City of Any City, County of Tour Way County, Texas, known as Your Where Dr (address/zip code), or as described on attached exhibit.

B. IMPROVEMENTS: The house, garage and all other fixtures and improvements attached to the above-described real property, including without limitation, the following **permanently installed and built-in items**, if any: all equipment and appliances, valances, screens, shutters, awnings, wall-to-wall carpeting, mirrors, ceiling fans, attic fans, mail boxes, television antennas, mounts and brackets for televisions and speakers, heating and air-conditioning units, security and fire detection equipment, wiring, plumbing and lighting fixtures, chandeliers, water softener system, kitchen equipment, garage door openers, cleaning equipment, shrubbery, landscaping, outdoor cooking equipment, and all other property attached to the above described real property.

C. ACCESSORIES: The following described related accessories, if any: window air conditioning units, stove, fireplace screens, curtains and rods, blinds, window shades, draperies and rods, door keys, mailbox keys, above ground pool, swimming pool equipment and maintenance accessories, artificial fireplace logs, security systems that are not fixtures, and controls for: (i) garage doors, (ii) entry gates, and (iii) other improvements and accessories. "Controls" includes Seller's transferable rights to the (i) software and applications used to access and control improvements or accessories, and (ii) hardware used solely to control improvements or accessories.

D. EXCLUSIONS: The following improvements and accessories will be retained by Seller and must be removed prior to delivery of possession: ____.

E. RESERVATIONS: Any reservation for oil, gas, or other minerals, water, timber, or other interests is made in accordance with an attached addendum.

3. SALES PRICE:

A. Cash portion of Sales Price payable by Buyer at closing .... $7,875.00. The term "Cash portion of the Sales Price" does not include proceeds from borrowing of any kind or selling other real property except as disclosed in this contract.

B. Sum of all financing described in the attached: ☒- Third Party Financing Addendum, Loan Assumption Addendum, Seller Financing Addendum .... $ 200,000.00

C. Sales Price (Sum of A and B) .... $ 207,875.00

4. LEASES: Except as disclosed in this contract, Seller is not aware of any leases affecting the Property. After the Effective Date, Seller may not, without Buyer's written consent, create a new lease, amend any existing lease, or convey any interest in the Property. (Check all applicable boxes)

A. RESIDENTIAL LEASES: The Property is subject to one or more residential leases and the Addendum Regarding Residential Leases is attached to this contract.

B. FIXTURE LEASES: Fixtures on the Property are subject to one or more fixture leases (for example, solar panels, propane tanks, water softener, security system) and the Addendum Regarding Fixture Leases is attached to this contract.

C. NATURAL RESOURCE LEASES: "Natural Resource Lease" means an existing oil and gas, mineral, geothermal, water, wind, or other natural resource lease affecting the Property to which Seller is a party.

(1) Seller has delivered to Buyer a copy of all the Natural Resource Leases.

(2) Seller has not delivered to Buyer a copy of all the Natural Resource Leases. Seller shall provide to Buyer a copy of all the Natural Resource Leases within 3 days after the Effective Date. Buyer may terminate the contract within ______ days after the date the Buyer receives all the Natural Resource Leases and the earnest money shall be refunded to Buyer.

5. EARNEST MONEY AND TERMINATION OPTION:

A. DELIVERY OF EARNEST MONEY AND OPTION FEE: Within 3 days after the Effective Date, Buyer must deliver to <u>Title Company</u> (Escrow Agent) at <u>1000 Purchase Street, Close My Deal, Tx 70002</u> (address): <u>$2,000.00</u> as earnest money and <u>$175.00</u> as the Option Fee. The earnest money and Option Fee shall be made payable to Escrow Agent and may be paid separately or combined in a single payment.

(1) Buyer shall deliver additional earnest money of $________days after the Effective Date of this contract. to Escrow Agent within______ days after the Effective Date of this contract.

(2) If the last day to deliver the earnest money, Option Fee, or the additional earnest money falls on a Saturday, Sunday, or legal holiday, the time to deliver the earnest money, Option Fee, or the additional earnest money, as applicable, is extended until the end of the next day that is not a Saturday, Sunday, or legal holiday.

(3) The amount(s) Escrow Agent receives under this paragraph shall be applied first to the Option Fee, then to the earnest money, and then to the additional earnest money.

(4) Buyer authorizes Escrow Agent to release and deliver the Option Fee to Seller at any time without further notice to or consent from Buyer, and releases Escrow Agent from liability for delivery of the Option Fee to Seller. The Option Fee will be credited to the Sales Price at closing.

B. TERMINATION OPTION: For nominal consideration, the receipt of which Seller acknowledges, and Buyer's agreement to pay the Option Fee within the time required, Seller grants Buyer the unrestricted right to terminate this contract by giving notice of termination to Seller within___7___ days after the Effective Date of this contract (Option Period). Notices under this paragraph must be given by 5:00 p.m. (local time where the Property is located) by the date specified. If Buyer gives notice of termination within the time prescribed: (i) the Option Fee will not be refunded and Escrow Agent shall release any Option Fee remaining with Escrow Agent to Seller; and (ii) any earnest money will be refunded to Buyer

C. FAILURE TO TIMELY DELIVER EARNEST MONEY: If Buyer fails to deliver the earnest money within the time required, Seller may terminate this contract or exercise Seller's remedies under Paragraph 15, or both, by providing notice to Buyer before Buyer delivers the earnest money.

D. FAILURE TO TIMELY DELIVER OPTION FEE: If no dollar amount is stated as the Option Fee or if Buyer fails to deliver the Option Fee within the time required, Buyer shall not have the unrestricted right to terminate this contract under this paragraph 5

E. TIME: **Time is of the essence for this paragraph and strict compliance with the time for performance is required.**

6. TITLE POLICY AND SURVEY:

A. TITLE POLICY: Seller shall furnish to Buyer at ☒ Seller's Buyer's expense an owner policy of title insurance (Title Policy) issued by Title Company (Title Company) in the amount of the Sales Price, dated at or after closing, insuring Buyer against loss under the provisions of the Title Policy, subject to the promulgated exclusions (including existing building and zoning ordinances) and the following exceptions:

(1) Restrictive covenants common to the platted subdivision in which the Property is located.

(2) The standard printed exception for standby fees, taxes and assessments.

(3) Liens created as part of the financing described in Paragraph 3.

(4) Utility easements created by the dedication deed or plat of the subdivision in which the Property is located.

(5) Reservations or exceptions otherwise permitted by this contract or as may be approved by Buyer in writing. (

(6) The standard printed exception as to marital rights.

(7) The standard printed exception as to waters, tidelands, beaches, streams, and related matters.

(8) The standard printed exception as to discrepancies, conflicts, shortages in area or boundary lines, encroachments or protrusions, or overlapping improvements:

(i) will not be amended or deleted from the title policy; or

(ii) will be amended to read, "shortages in area" at the expense of Buyer Seller.

(9) The exception or exclusion regarding minerals approved by the Texas Department of Insurance.

B. COMMITMENT: Within 20 days after the Title Company receives a copy of this contract, Seller shall furnish to Buyer a commitment for title insurance (Commitment) and, at Buyer's expense, legible copies of restrictive covenants and documents evidencing exceptions in the Commitment (Exception Documents) other than the standard printed exceptions. Seller authorizes the Title Company to deliver the Commitment and Exception Documents to Buyer at Buyer's address shown in Paragraph 21. If the Commitment and Exception Documents are not delivered to Buyer within the specified time, the time for delivery will be automatically extended up to 15 days or 3 days before the Closing Date, whichever is earlier. If the Commitment and Exception Documents are not delivered within the time required, Buyer may terminate this contract and the earnest money will be refunded to Buyer.

C. SURVEY: The survey must be made by a registered professional land surveyor acceptable to the Title Company and Buyer's lender(s). (Check one box only)

(1) Within ____ days after the Effective Date of this contract, Seller shall furnish to Buyer and Title Company Seller's existing survey of the Property and a Residential Real Property Affidavit or Declaration promulgated by the Texas Department of Insurance (T-47 Affidavit or T-47.1 Declaration). Buyer shall obtain a new survey at Seller's expense no later than 3 days prior to Closing Date if Seller

fails to furnish within the time prescribed both the: (i) existing survey; and (ii) affidavit or declaration. If the Title Company or Buyer's lender does not accept the existing survey, or the affidavit or declaration, Buyer shall obtain a new survey at Seller's Buyer's expense no later than 3 days prior to Closing Date.

(2) Within ____ days after the Effective Date of this contract, Buyer may obtain a new survey at Buyer's expense. Buyer is deemed to receive the survey on the date of actual receipt or the date specified in this paragraph, whichever is earlier. If Buyer fails to obtain the survey, Buyer may not terminate the contract under Paragraph 2B of the Third Party Financing Addendum because the survey was not obtained.

(3) Within days after the Effective Date of this contract, Seller, at Seller's expense shall furnish a new survey to Buyer.

D. OBJECTIONS: Buyer may object in writing to defects, exceptions, or encumbrances to title: disclosed on the survey other than items 6A(1) through (7) above; disclosed in the Commitment other than items 6A(1) through (9) above; or which prohibit the following use or activity: ____

__. Buyer must object the earlier of (i) the Closing Date or (ii) _____ days after Buyer receives the Commitment, Exception Documents, and the survey. Buyer's failure to object within the time allowed will constitute a waiver of

Buyer's right to object; except that the requirements in Schedule C of the Commitment are not waived by Buyer. Provided Seller is not obligated to incur any expense, Seller shall cure any timely objections of Buyer or any third party lender within 15 days after Seller receives the objections (Cure Period) and the Closing Date will be extended as necessary. If objections are not cured within the Cure Period, Buyer may, by delivering notice to Seller within 5 days after the end of the Cure Period: (i) terminate this contract and the earnest money will be refunded to Buyer; or (ii) waive the objections. If Buyer does not terminate within the time required, Buyer shall be deemed to have waived the objections. If the Commitment or survey is revised or any new Exception Document(s) is delivered, Buyer may object to any new matter revealed in the revised Commitment or survey or new Exception Document(s) within the same time stated in this paragraph to make objections beginning when the revised Commitment, survey, or Exception Document(s) is delivered to Buyer

E. TITLE NOTICES:

1. ABSTRACT OR TITLE POLICY: Broker advises Buyer to have an abstract of title covering the Property examined by an attorney of Buyer's selection, or Buyer should be furnished with or obtain a Title Policy. If a Title Policy is furnished, the Commitment should be promptly reviewed by

an attorney of Buyer's choice due to the time limitations on Buyer's right to object.

(2) MEMBERSHIP IN PROPERTY OWNERS ASSOCIATION(S): The Property is is not subject to mandatory membership in a property owners association(s). If the Property is subject to mandatory membership in a property owners association(s), Seller notifies Buyer under §5.012, Texas Property Code, that, as a purchaser of property in the residential community identified in Paragraph 2A in which the Property is located, you are obligated to be a member of the property owners association(s). Restrictive covenants governing the use and occupancy of the Property and all dedicatory instruments governing the establishment, maintenance, or operation of this residential community have been or will be recorded in the Real Property Records of the county in which the Property is located. Copies of the restrictive covenants and dedicatory instruments may be obtained from the county clerk. **You are obligated to pay assessments to the property owners association(s). The amount of the assessments is subject to change. Your failure to pay the assessments could result in enforcement of the association's lien on and the foreclosure of the Property.**

Section 207.003, Property Code, entitles an owner to receive copies of any document that governs the establishment, maintenance, or operation of a subdivision, including, but not limited to, restrictions, bylaws, rules and regulations, and a resale certificate from a property owners' association. A resale certificate contains information including, but not limited to, statements specifying the amount and frequency of regular assessments and the style and cause number of lawsuits to which the property owners' association is a party, other than lawsuits relating to unpaid ad valorem taxes of an individual member of the association. These documents must be made available to you by the property owners' association or the association's agent on your request. **If Buyer is concerned about these matters, the TREC promulgated Addendum for Property Subject to Mandatory Membership in a Property Owners Association(s) should be used.**

(3) STATUTORY TAX DISTRICTS: If the Property is situated in a utility or other statutorily created district providing water, sewer, drainage, or flood control facilities and services, Chapter 49, Texas Water Code, requires Seller to deliver and Buyer to sign the statutory notice relating to the tax rate, bonded indebtedness, or standby fee of the district prior to final execution of this contract.

(4) TIDE WATERS: If the Property abuts the tidally influenced waters of the state, §33.135, Texas Natural Resources Code, requires a notice regarding coastal area property to be included in the contract. An addendum

containing the notice promulgated by TREC or required by the parties must be used.

(5) ANNEXATION: If the Property is located outside the limits of a municipality, Seller notifies Buyer under §5.011, Texas Property Code, that the Property may now or later be included in the extraterritorial jurisdiction of a municipality and may now or later be subject to annexation by the municipality. Each municipality maintains a map that depicts its boundaries and extraterritorial jurisdiction. To determine if the Property is located within a municipality's extraterritorial jurisdiction or is likely to be located within a municipality's extraterritorial jurisdiction, contact all municipalities located in the general proximity of the Property for further information.

(6) PROPERTY LOCATED IN A CERTIFICATED SERVICE AREA OF A UTILITY SERVICE PROVIDER: Notice required by §13.257, Water Code: The real property, described in Paragraph 2, that you are about to purchase may be located in a certificated water or sewer service area, which is authorized by law to provide water or sewer service to the properties in the certificated area. If your property is located in a certificated area there may be special costs or charges that you will be required to pay before you can receive water or sewer service. There may be a period required to construct lines or other facilities necessary to provide water or sewer service to your property. You are advised to determine if the

property is in a certificated area and contact the utility service provider to determine the cost that you will be required to pay and the period, if any, that is required to provide water or sewer service to your property. The undersigned Buyer hereby acknowledges receipt of the foregoing notice at or before the execution of a binding contract for the purchase of the real property described in Paragraph 2 or at closing of purchase of the real property.

(7) PUBLIC IMPROVEMENT DISTRICTS: If the Property is in a public improvement district, Seller must give Buyer written notice as required by §5.014, Property Code. An addendum containing the required notice shall be attached to this contract.

(8) TRANSFER FEES: If the Property is subject to a private transfer fee obligation, §5.205, Property Code, requires Seller to notify Buyer as follows: The private transfer fee obligation may be governed by Chapter 5, Subchapter G of the Texas Property Code.

(9) PROPANE GAS SYSTEM SERVICE AREA: If the Property is located in a propane gas system service area owned by a distribution system retailer, Seller must give Buyer written notice as required by §141.010, Texas Utilities Code. An addendum containing the notice approved by TREC or required by the parties should be used.

(10) NOTICE OF WATER LEVEL FLUCTUATIONS: If the Property adjoins an impoundment of water, including a

reservoir or lake, constructed and maintained under Chapter 11, Water Code, that has a storage capacity of at least 5,000 acre-feet at the impoundment's normal operating level, Seller hereby notifies Buyer: "The water level of the impoundment of water adjoining the Property fluctuates for various reasons, including as a result of: (1) an entity lawfully exercising its right to use the water stored in the impoundment; or (2) drought or flood conditions."

(11) CERTIFICATE OF MOLD REMEDIATION: If the Property has been remediated for mold, Seller must provide to Buyer each certificate of mold damage remediation issued under §1958.154, Occupations Code, during the 5 years preceding the sale of the Property.

(12) REQUIRED NOTICES: The following notices have been given or are attached to this contract (for example, utility, water, drainage, and public improvement districts): ______MUD (Maybe)______ Seller's failure to provide applicable statutory notices may provide Buyer with remedies or rights to terminate the contract.

7. PROPERTYCONDITION:

A. ACCESS, INSPECTIONS AND UTILITIES: Seller shall permit Buyer and Buyer's agents access to the Property at reasonable times. Buyer may have the Property inspected by inspectors selected by Buyer and licensed by TREC or otherwise permitted by law to make inspections. Any hydrostatic testing must be separately authorized by Seller in writing. Seller at Seller's expense shall immediately cause existing utilities to be turned on and shall keep the utilities on during the time this contract is in effect.

B. SELLER'S DISCLOSURE NOTICE PURSUANT TO§5.008, TEXAS PROPERTY CODE (Notice):

(Check one box only)

(1) Buyer has received the Notice.

(2) Buyer has not received the Notice. Within ______ days after the Effective Date of this contract, Seller shall deliver the Notice to Buyer. If Buyer does not receive the Notice, Buyer may terminate this contract at any time prior to the closing and the earnest money will be refunded to Buyer. If Seller delivers the Notice, Buyer may terminate this contract for any reason within 7 days after Buyer receives the Notice or prior to the closing, whichever first occurs, and the earnest money will be refunded to Buyer.

(3) The Seller is not required to furnish the notice under the Texas Property Code.

C. SELLER'S DISCLOSURE OF LEAD-BASED PAINT AND LEAD-BASED PAINT HAZARDS is required by Federal law for a residential dwelling constructed prior to 1978.

D. ACCEPTANCE OF PROPERTY CONDITION: "As Is" means the present condition of the Property with any and all defects and without warranty except for the warranties of title and the warranties in this contract. Buyer's agreement to accept the Property As Is under Paragraph 7D(1) or (2) does not preclude Buyer from inspecting the Property under Paragraph 7A, from negotiating repairs or treatments in a subsequent amendment, or from terminating this contract during the Option Period, if any.

(Check one box only)

(1) Buyer accepts the Property As Is.

(2) Buyer accepts the Property As Is provided Seller, at Seller's expense, shall complete the following specific repairs and treatments: ______________________________

____

(Do not insert general phrases, such as "subject to inspections" that do not identify specific repairs and treatments.)

E. LENDER REQUIRED REPAIRS AND TREATMENTS: Unless otherwise agreed in writing, neither party is obligated to pay for lender required repairs, which includes treatment for wood destroying insects. If the parties do not agree to pay for the lender required repairs or treatments, this contract will terminate and the earnest money will be refunded to Buyer. If the cost of lender required repairs and treatments exceeds 5% of the Sales Price, Buyer may terminate this contract and the earnest money will be refunded to Buyer.

F. COMPLETION OF REPAIRS AND TREATMENTS: Unless otherwise agreed in writing, Seller shall complete all agreed repairs and treatments prior to the Closing Date and obtain any required permits. The repairs and treatments must be performed by persons who are licensed to provide such repairs or treatments or, if no license is required by law, are commercially engaged in the trade of providing such repairs or treatments. Seller shall: (i) provide Buyer with copies of documentation from the repair person(s) showing the scope of work and payment for the work completed; and (ii) at Seller's expense, arrange for the transfer of any transferable warranties with respect to the repairs and treatments to Buyer at closing. If Seller fails to complete any agreed repairs and treatments prior to the Closing Date, Buyer may exercise remedies under Paragraph 15 or extend the Closing Date up to 5 days if necessary for Seller to complete the repairs and treatments.

G. ENVIRONMENTAL MATTERS: Buyer is advised that the presence of wetlands, toxic substances, including asbestos and wastes or other environmental hazards, or the presence of a threatened or endangered species or its habitat may affect Buyer's intended use of the Property. If Buyer is concerned about these matters, an addendum promulgated by TREC or required by the parties should be used.

H. RESIDENTIAL SERVICE CONTRACTS: Buyer may purchase a residential service contract from a provider or administrator licensed by the Texas Department of Licensing and Regulation. If Buyer purchases a residential service contract, Seller shall reimburse Buyer at closing for the cost of the residential service contract in an amount not exceeding ___$475.00___. Buyer should review any residential service contract for the scope of coverage, exclusions and limitations. **The purchase of a residential service contract is optional. Similar coverage may be purchased from various companies authorized to do business in Texas.**

8. BROKERSANDSALESAGENTS:

A. BROKER OR SALES AGENT DISCLOSURE: Texas law requires a real estate broker or sales agent who is a party to a transaction or acting on behalf of a spouse, parent, child, business entity in which the broker or sales agent owns more than 10%, or a trust for which the broker or sales agent acts as a trustee or of which the broker or sales agent or the broker or sales agent's spouse, parent or child is a beneficiary, to notify the other party in writing before entering into a contract of sale. Disclose if applicable:____

____

____

B. BROKERS' FEES: All obligations of the parties for payment of brokers' fees are contained in separate written agreements.

9. CLOSING:

A. The closing of the sale will be on or before __**Neverary**__ , ____________________ , _________________ or within 7 days after objections made under Paragraph 6D have been cured or waived, whichever date is later (Closing Date). If either party fails to close the sale by the Closing Date, the non-defaulting party may exercise the remedies contained in Paragraph 15.

B. At closing:

(1) Seller shall execute and deliver a general warranty deed conveying title to the Property to Buyer and showing no additional exceptions to those permitted in Paragraph 6 and furnish tax statements or certificates showing no delinquent taxes on the Property.

(2) Buyer shall pay the Sales Price in good funds acceptable to the Escrow Agent.

(3) Seller and Buyer shall execute and deliver any notices, statements, certificates, affidavits, releases, loan documents, transfer of any warranties, and other documents reasonably required for the closing of the sale and the issuance of the Title Policy.

(4) There will be no liens, assessments, or security interests against the Property which will not be satisfied out of the sales proceeds unless securing the payment of any loans assumed by Buyer and assumed loans will not be in default.

(5) Private transfer fees (as defined by Chapter 5, Subchapter G of the Texas Property Code) will be the obligation of Seller unless provided otherwise in this contract. Transfer fees assessed by a property owners' association are governed by the Addendum for Property Subject to Mandatory Membership in a Property Owners Association.

10. POSSESSION:

A. BUYER'SPOSSESSION: Seller shall deliver to Buyer possession of the Property in its present or required condition, ordinary wear and tear excepted: ☐ upon closing and funding according to a temporary residential lease form promulgated by TREC or other written lease required by the parties. Any possession by Buyer prior to closing or by Seller after closing which is not authorized by a written lease will establish a tenancy at sufferance relationship between the parties. **Consult your insurance agent prior to change of ownership and possession because insurance coverage may be limited or terminated. The absence of a written lease or appropriate insurance coverage may expose the parties to economic loss.**

B. SMART DEVICES: "Smart Device" means a device that connects to the internet to enable remote use, monitoring, and management of: (i) the Property; (ii) items identified in any Non Realty Items Addendum; or (iii) items in a Fixture Lease assigned to Buyer. At the time Seller delivers possession of the Property to Buyer, Seller shall:

(1) deliver to Buyer written information containing all access codes, usernames, passwords, and applications Buyer will need to access, operate, manage, and control the Smart Devices; and

(2) terminate and remove all access and connections to the improvements and accessories from any of Seller's personal devices including but not limited to phones and computers.

11. SPECIAL PROVISIONS: (This paragraph is intended to be used only for additional informational items. An informational item is a statement that completes a blank in a contract form, discloses factual information, or provides instructions. Real estate brokers and sales agents are prohibited from practicing law and shall not add to, delete, or modify any provision of this contract unless drafted by a party to this contract or a party's attorney.)______________

____

____

12. SETTLEMENT AND OTHER EXPENSES:

A. The following expenses must be paid at or prior to closing:

(1) Seller shall pay the following expenses (Seller's Expenses):

(a) releases of existing liens, including prepayment penalties and recording fees; release of Seller's loan liability; tax statements or certificates; preparation of deed; one-half of escrow fee; brokerage fees that Seller has agreed to pay; and other expenses payable by Seller under this contract;

(b) the following amount to be applied to brokerage fees that Buyer has agreed to pay: $____________ or ___2.5___% of the Sales Price (check one box only); and

(c) an amount not to exceed ___$6,700.00___ to be applied to other Buyer's Expenses.

(2) Buyer shall pay the following expenses (Buyer's Expenses): Appraisal fees; loan application fees; origination charges; credit reports; preparation of loan documents; interest on the notes from date of disbursement to one month prior to dates of first monthly payments; recording fees; copies of easements and restrictions; loan title policy with endorsements required by lender; loan-related inspection fees; photos; amortization schedules; one-half of escrow fee; all prepaid items, including required premiums for flood and hazard insurance, reserve deposits for insurance, ad valorem taxes and special governmental assessments; final compliance inspection; courier fee; repair inspection; underwriting fee; wire transfer fee; expenses incident to any loan; Private Mortgage Insurance Premium (PMI), VA Loan Funding Fee, or FHA Mortgage Insurance Premium (MIP) as required by the lender; brokerage fees that Buyer has agreed to pay; and other expenses payable by Buyer under this contract.

B. If any expense exceeds an amount expressly stated in this contract for such expense to be paid by a party, that party may terminate this contract unless the other party agrees to pay such excess. Buyer may not pay charges and fees expressly prohibited by FHA, VA, Texas Veterans Land Board or other governmental loan program regulations.

13. PRORATIONS: Taxes for the current year, interest, rents, and regular periodic maintenance fees, assessments, and dues (including prepaid items) will be prorated through the Closing Date. The tax proration may be calculated taking into consideration any change in exemptions that will affect the current year's taxes. If taxes for the current year vary from the amount prorated at closing, the parties shall adjust the prorations when tax statements for the current year are available. If taxes are not paid at or prior to closing, Buyer shall pay taxes for the current year.

14. CASUALTY LOSS: If any part of the Property is damaged or destroyed by fire or other casualty after the Effective Date of this contract, Seller shall restore the Property to its previous condition as soon as reasonably possible, but in any event by the Closing Date. If Seller fails to do so due to factors beyond Seller's control, Buyer may (a) terminate this contract and the earnest money will be refunded to Buyer (b) extend the time for performance up to 15 days and the Closing Date will be extended as necessary or (c) accept the Property in its damaged condition with an assignment of insurance proceeds, if permitted by Seller's insurance carrier, and receive credit from Seller at closing in the amount of the deductible under the insurance policy. Seller's obligations under this paragraph are independent of any other obligations of Seller under this contract.

15. DEFAULT: If Buyer fails to comply with this contract, Buyer will be in default, and Seller may (a) enforce specific performance, seek such other relief as may be provided by law, or both, or (b) terminate this contract and receive the earnest money as liquidated damages, thereby releasing both parties from this contract. If Seller fails to comply with this contract, Seller will be in default and Buyer may (a) enforce specific performance, seek such other relief as may be provided by law, or both, or (b) terminate this contract and receive the earnest money, thereby releasing both parties from this contract.

16. MEDIATION: It is the policy of the State of Texas to encourage resolution of disputes through alternative dispute resolution procedures such as mediation. Any dispute between Seller and Buyer related to this contract which is not resolved through informal discussion will be submitted to a mutually acceptable mediation service or provider. The parties to the mediation shall bear the mediation costs equally. This paragraph does not preclude a party from seeking equitable relief from a court of competent jurisdiction.

17. ATTORNEY'S FEES: A Buyer, Seller, Listing Broker, Other Broker, or Escrow Agent who prevails in any legal proceeding related to this contract is entitled to recover reasonable attorney's fees and all costs of such proceeding.

18. ESCROW:

A. ESCROW: The Escrow Agent is not (i) a party to this contract and does not have liability for the performance or nonperformance of any party to this contract, (ii) liable for interest on the earnest money and (iii) liable for the loss of any earnest money caused by the failure of any financial institution in which the earnest money has been deposited unless the financial institution is acting as Escrow Agent. Escrow Agent may require any disbursement made in connection with this contract to be conditioned on Escrow Agent's collection of good funds acceptable to Escrow Agent.

B. EXPENSES: At closing, the earnest money must be applied first to any cash down payment, then to Buyer's Expenses and any excess refunded to Buyer. If no closing occurs, Escrow Agent may: (i) require a written release of liability of the Escrow Agent from all parties before releasing any earnest money; and (ii) require payment of unpaid expenses incurred on behalf of a party. Escrow Agent may deduct authorized expenses from the earnest money payable to a party. "Authorized expenses" means expenses incurred by Escrow Agent on behalf of the party entitled to the earnest money that were authorized by this contract or that party.

C. DEMAND: Upon termination of this contract, either party or the Escrow Agent may send a release of earnest money to each party and the parties shall execute counterparts of the release and deliver same to the Escrow Agent. If either party fails to execute the release, either party may make a written demand to the Escrow Agent for the earnest money. If only one party makes written demand for the earnest money, Escrow Agent shall promptly provide a copy of the demand to the other party. If Escrow Agent does not receive written objection to the demand from the other party within 15 days, Escrow Agent may disburse the earnest money to the party making demand reduced by the amount of unpaid expenses incurred on behalf of the party receiving the earnest money and Escrow Agent may pay the same to the creditors. If Escrow Agent complies with the provisions of this paragraph, each party hereby releases Escrow Agent from all adverse claims related to the disbursal of the earnest money.

D. DAMAGES: Any party who wrongfully fails or refuses to sign a release acceptable to the Escrow Agent within 7 days of receipt of the request will be liable to the other party for (i) damages; (ii) the earnest money; (iii) reasonable attorney's fees; and (iv) all costs of suit.

E. NOTICES: Escrow Agent's notices will be effective when sent in compliance with Paragraph 21. Notice of objection to the demand will be deemed effective upon receipt by Escrow Agent.

19. REPRESENTATIONS: All covenants, representations and warranties in this contract survive closing. If any representation of Seller in this contract is untrue on the Closing Date, Seller will be in default. Unless expressly prohibited by written agreement, Seller may continue to show the Property and receive, negotiate and accept back up offers.

20. FEDERAL REQUIREMENTS: If Seller is a "foreign person," as defined by Internal Revenue Code and its regulations, or if Seller fails to deliver an affidavit or a certificate of non-foreign status to Buyer that Seller is not a "foreign person," then Buyer shall withhold from the sales proceeds an amount sufficient to comply with applicable tax law and deliver the same to the Internal Revenue Service together with appropriate tax forms. Internal Revenue Service regulations require filing written reports if currency in excess of specified amounts is received in the transaction.

21. NOTICES: All notices from one party to the other must be in writing and are effective when mailed to, hand-delivered at, or transmitted by fax or electronic transmission as follows:

To Buyer at: ______________	To Seller ______________
______________ ______________	______________ ______________
Phone: ______________	Phone: ______________
E-mail/Fax: ______________ ______________	E-mail/Fax: ______________ ______________
E-mail/Fax: ______________ ______________	E-mail/Fax: ______________ ______________
With a copy to Buyer's agent at: ______________ ______________	With a copy to Buyer's agent at: ______________ ______________

22. AGREEMENT OF PARTIES: This contract contains the entire agreement of the parties and cannot be changed except by their written agreement. Addenda which are a part of this contract are (Check all applicable boxes):

- [x] Third Party Financing Addendum
- [ ] Seller Financing Addendum
- [ ] Addendum for Property Subject to Mandatory Membership in a Property Owners Association
- [ ] Buyer's Temporary Residential Lease
- [ ] Loan Assumption Addendum
- [ ] Addendum for Sale of Other Property by Buyer
- [ ] Addendum for Reservation of Oil, Gas and Other Minerals
- [ ] Addendum for "Back-Up" Contract
- [ ] Addendum for Coastal Area Property
- [ ] Addendum for Authorizing Hydrostatic Testing
- [ ] Addendum Concerning Right to Terminate Due to Lender's Appraisal
- [ ] Environmental Assessment, Threatened or Endangered Species and Wetlands Addendum
- [ ] Seller's Temporary Residential Lease
- [ ] Short Sale Addendum
- [ ] Addendum for Property Located Seaward of the Gulf Intracoastal Waterway
- [ ] Addendum for Seller's Disclosure of Information on Lead-based Paint and Lead-based Paint Hazards as Required by Federal Law
- [ ] Addendum for Property in a Propane Gas System Service Area
- [ ] Addendum Regarding Residential Leases
- [ ] Addendum Regarding Fixture Leases
- [ ] Addendum containing Notice of Obligation to Pay Improvement District Assessment
- [ ] Addendum for Section 1031 Exchange
- [x] Other (list): **Down Payment Assistance Program**

23. CONSULT AN ATTORNEY BEFORE SIGNING: TREC rules prohibit real estate brokers and sales agents from giving legal advice. READ THIS CONTRACT CAREFULLY.

Buyer Attorney is ____________	Seller's Attorney is ____________
Phone: ____________	Phone: ____________
Fax: ____________	Fax: ____________
E-mail: ____________	E-mail: ____________

EXECUTED the __________ day of ___________, 20______ (Effective Date). (BROKER: FILL IN THE DATE OF FINAL ACCEPTANCE.)

______________________________	______________________________
Buyer For Educational Purposes ONLY	Buyer For Educational Purposes ONLY

______________________________	______________________________
Buyer	Seller

The form of this contract has been approved by the Texas Real Estate Commission. TREC forms are intended for use only by trained real estate license holders. No representation is made as to the legal validity or adequacy of any provision in any specific transactions. It is not intended for complex transactions. Texas Real Estate Commission, P.O. Box 12188, Austin, TX 78711-2188, (512) 936-3000 (http://www.trec.texas.gov) TREC NO .20-18.This form replaces TREC NO.20-17.

BROKER INFORMATION

(Print name(s) only. Do not sign)

Realtor's Firm Other Broker Firm — License No.	**Other Realtor's Firm** Listing Broker Firm — License No.
represents [X] Buyer only as Buyer's agent [ ] Seller as Listing Broker's subagent	represents [ ] Seller and Buyer as an intermediary [X] Seller only as Seller's agent
Buyer's Agent Associate's Name — License No.	**Seller's Agent** Listing Associate's Name — License No.
Team Name	Team Name
Associate's Email Address — Phone	Listing Associate's Email Address — Phone
Licensed Supervisor of Associate — License No.	Licensed Supervisor of Listing Associate — License No.
Other Broker's Address — Phone	Listing Broker's Office Address — Phone
City — State — Zip	City — State — Zip
	Selling Associate's Name — License No.
	Team Name
	Selling Associate's Email Address — Phone
	Licensed Supervisor of Selling Associate — License No.
	Selling Associate's Office Address
	City — State — Zip

Disclosure: Pursuant to a previous, separate agreement, Listing Broker has agreed to pay Other Broker a fee ([ ] $ or [X] - 3000 % of the Sales Price). This disclosure is for informational purposes and does not change the previous agreement between brokers to pay or share a commission.

OPTION FEE RECEIPT

Receipt of $__________________ (Option Fee) in the form of __________________________________
is acknowledged.

Escrow Agent **Title Company** ______________________ Date

EARNEST MONEY RECEIPT

Receipt of $__________________ Earnest Money in the form of __________________________________
is acknowledged.

Escrow Agent ______ Received by ______ Email Address ______ Date/Time

Address ______ Phone

City ______ State ______ Zip ______ Fax

CONTRACT RECEIPT

Receipt of the Contract is acknowledged.

Escrow Agent ______ Received by ______ Email Address ______ Date

Address ______ Phone

City ______ State ______ Zip ______ Fax

ADDITIONAL EARNEST MONEY RECEIPT

Receipt of $__________________ additional Earnest Money in the form of __________________________
is acknowledged.

Escrow Agent ______ Received by ______ Email Address ______ Date/Time

Address ______ Phone

City ______ State ______ Zip ______ Fax

Vanterpool Real Estate Co., 1803 Lauren Place Missouri City TX 77489 **Phone:** 5049753931 **Fax:** Kayla Carter

Zenobia Pressley Produced with Lone Wolf Transactions (zip Form Edition) 717 N Harwood St, Suite 2200, Dallas, TX 75201. www.lwolf.com

Settlement Statement/Closing Disclosure

LOAN & TRANSACTION DETAILS

Item	Description	Amount
Sales Price	Purchase price of the home	$250,000
Loan Amount	FHA loan provided by the lender	$245,000
Down Payment	Buyer's portion (3.5%)	$5,000
Earnest Money Deposit	Paid upfront and applied to total	–$1,500
Seller Credit	Contribution to buyer's closing costs	–$2,000
Cash to Close (Final)	Buyer must bring to closing	$11,995

BUYER'S CLOSING COSTS

- Loan Origination Fee: lender charge for processing — $1,000
- Appraisal Fee: required by lender — $550

- Credit Report Fee: pulled during application — $45
- Flood Certification: if applicable — $20
- Title Insurance: owner's and lender's policy — $850
- Settlement Agent Fee: charged by title company — $500
- Recording Fees: county document fees — $200
- Prepaid Property Taxes: for escrow (3 months) — $900
- Homeowners Insurance: first year premium — $1,200
- Daily Interest (15 days): mortgage interest until first payment — $375
- Escrow Reserves: 2 months taxes and insurance — $1,500

Total Buyer Closing Costs: $7,140

Seller's Closing Costs

- Real Estate Commission: 6% (split between buyer and seller agents) — $15,000
- Title Company Fees: split with buyer — $500
- Property Taxes Owed: prorated to closing — $600

Total Seller Costs: $16,100

Summary – Buyer's Side

- Total Due from Buyer at Closing: $250,000 (purchase) + $7,140 (costs) = $257,140
- Less Loan Amount: –$245,000
- Less Earnest Money: –$1,500
- Less Seller Credit: –$2,000

Final Cash to Close: $8,640

Pro Tip:

"Your Closing Disclosure must be given to you at least 3 business days before closing. Review it line by line with your lender or agent, and don't be afraid to ask questions. This is your money!"

About The Author

Zee Pressley, widely known as *Just Ask Zee*, is a licensed Realtor, certified teacher, and self-growth enthusiast with a passion for helping everyday people take powerful steps toward homeownership and financial freedom. Since 2006, Zee has taught free homebuyer classes, worked hands-on with small businesses, and built a reputation as the go-to person for real talk and real results.

She holds a bachelor's degree in Business Management and a master's in Mental Wellness, specializing in family dynamics—making her uniquely equipped to guide clients through both the financial and emotional milestones of buying a home. Her client base spans Texas and beyond, thanks to her national referral network and popular online workshops.

Zee's friends and colleagues know her as the person who gives you the information you *didn't know you needed*—with a warm smile, a sharp wit, and a whole lot of heart. She believes that most people don't pursue homeownership because no one ever showed them how simple and possible it can be. *Dream Key* is her invitation to change that.

When she's not writing or working with clients, you'll find her walking 5 miles a day for her mental and physical health, reading books that stretch her perspective, and laughing her way through life—usually with a strong cup of coffee in hand.

www.ingramcontent.com/pod-product-compliance
Lightning Source LLC
LaVergne TN
LVHW022042200926
848481LV00003B/745
9798349598326